Heaven Is Beautiful

Heaven Is Beautiful

....

How Dying Taught Me That
Death Is Just the Beginning

PETER BALDWIN PANAGORE

HarperCollins*Publishers*Ltd

Heaven Is Beautiful
Copyright © 2015 by Peter Baldwin Panagore

Published by HarperCollins Publishers Ltd, by arrangement with
Hampton Roads Publishing Company

First Canadian edition

HarperCollins books may be purchased for educational, business,
or sales promotional use through our Special Markets Department.

HarperCollins Publishers Ltd
2 Bloor Street East, 20th Floor
Toronto, Ontario, Canada
M4W 1A8

www.harpercollins.ca

Library and Archives Canada Cataloguing in Publication
information is available upon request

ISBN 978-1-44344-664-8

Printed and bound in the United States of America
RRD 9 8 7 6 5 4 3 2 1

For Mom and Dad

Contents

Lower Weeping Wall on Cirrus Mountain, Banff National Park, Alberta, Canada, where the author died, crossed over, and then came back to life. Photograph by Peter Valchev.

We are not human beings having a
spiritual experience; we are spiritual
beings having a human experience.

—Pierre Teilhard de Chardin

Introduction

"My thoughts are nothing like your thoughts," says the Lord. "And my ways are far beyond anything you could imagine."

—Isaiah 55:8 (NLT)

This is the story of how I died, why I came back, and what has become of me since.

Dying changed my life forever. I am not the same person I was before that transformative night. There are a hundred times that I wish and pray it had never happened. But it did, on March 20, 1980. I was stuck on a mountain, stranded in the wilderness, in the bitter cold, with no way down. Only by the grace of God am I here today.

The first time I told my story was five years after my accident, in 1985, to my bride-to-be on the night before our wedding. *Better late than never,* I thought. I had struggled with telling her but finally decided she needed to know what she was getting into before she married me.

After that, I never told another person—until my friend Bryan witnessed an incident in my presence.

I was the only trained responder at the scene of a bad car wreck, and I prayed over one of the men whose injuries were internal, which meant that the only thing I could do was to treat him for shock and pray. Suddenly a bolt of electricity surged through me repeatedly and into the man I was caring for. I did not know what was happening, only that somehow I was a conduit for the power of God.

Once we were back in our car driving south again, all of a sudden all the pain suffered by the accident victim was inexplicably transferred to me. I writhed and screamed in agony and screamed for many minutes, much to my friend's disconcertion and fear, until I felt and "saw" a cross that was atop a steeple by the side of the highway leap at me and somehow strike me. Just as suddenly, the pain vanished.

I know how kooky this sounds and looked to my friend. This happened when we were in divinity school together in 1986, and afterward, I felt I had to explain myself; so I told him my tale.

It wasn't until a Sunday in 2001 that I spoke of my near-death experience (NDE) again. I was the minister of the Congregational Church of Boothbay Harbor, Maine, and our community was going through great hardship. We had suffered through ten years of embezzlement by a church member and incredible fallout due to it. The people of the church were stressed, anxious, and exhausted. On one Sunday morning, just before church, a parishioner asked me "how my faith had endured unshakably" through a decade of church turmoil. His question made me stop in my tracks. He asked about my faith, and

Heaven Is Beautiful

for the first time I understood the profound shift within myself. My faith? What near-death experiencer has need of faith when he *knows* God is Real? I realized it was time to finally tell my congregants the truth about who I was. Right then and there I scrapped the sermon I'd spent half a week on and stood in the pulpit, ready to share my story and why I would say I have no faith.

Alarming words to read, I know, especially coming from the mouth of a Christian minister. But that is the plain truth. My faith in God did not sustain me in the pulpit through the dark times in our church. I was sustained by something else, by something that I had learned when I died: *I know that I am known by God* and *I know that God is Real.*

In the same way that I don't believe in snow or birds or trees because I can see them and experience them with my all of my senses, knowing they're real, I do not have to "believe" in God, because God is Real. God is as real to me as snow or birds or trees. Truly, God is more Real to me than any of those things. God is the only Real there is—and that is what this story is all about.

Since finally sharing my NDE story from the pulpit that Sunday morning to a surprised and appreciative congregation, I stopped holding it in. It was time to be honest about my newfound understanding of the Realness of God. My church and I had suffered greatly during that decade of embezzlement; yet through that dark time God was always with me, and is with me now inescapably—not because of who I am, but because of who God is. I told my story publicly that first time to help my congregation begin the healing process.

Since then, I have told my story to audiences large and small, to individuals over coffee, to the terminally ill, to the grieving, and from coast to coast. I am thankful to God that in my ministry, my death and return to life have turned me into something of a reverse midwife. Instead of catching babies as they enter this world, I've eased the passage of the dying into the next and much more beautiful world.

I tell my story not to ease the dying process, for dying, I have seen so many times, can be terribly painful, or quietly peaceful, or shockingly sudden. I tell my story here for the reasons that I always tell it: to give hope that is stronger than death, to give courage to the fearful, to give faith to the wavering and faithless, to take the sting from death, to ease grief, to teach that love is eternal and that beauty beyond words awaits us all on the other side. And, I also tell it to help those like me who have had a near-death experience to find their voice, to speak their truth, and to know what I did not, and could not, know for decades: *You are not alone.* There are many like us. More and more of us return each day through the miracles of modern medicine.

Let me add that like all NDEers, there has always been a volcano in my soul to speak about this, and there still is. The strange thing is that the more I've thought about that experience in the wilderness over the decades, the more details I remember. To date, this is the clearest account. There is a saying attributed to Pierre Teilhard de Chardin that captures my inner space, the center of my experience where I live today and have lived since that day in March of 1980: "We are not human beings having a spiritual experience. We are spiritual beings having a human experience." I am proof of that.

Fear not. God is with us, intimately and personally, immanent and transcendent, and God will catch each of us because God loves each of us as if we are God's only beloved. God will catch us when the door of death opens to swallow us whole, and wholly, and we depart this shell of flesh and bone and find ourselves in the inexplicable beauty and love of God's eternal Home prepared for us.

The author two years after his near-death experience, atop the summit marker on Mount Madison in White Mountain National Forest, New Hampshire, 1982. Photograph by Don Scott.

*Here is a test to find whether
your mission on earth is finished:
If you're alive, it isn't.*

—Richard Bach, *Illusions*

❦ 1 ❦

Goat Foot Boys Get Gear

The first time I met Tim, I was walking the five or so blocks from my off-campus room over to the student lounge on the Montana State University campus, in Bozeman, where I was a national exchange student for the year. It was a sunny, polar-cold afternoon with a near gale blowing down from the north, and we wanted to talk about spring break. For weeks I had been trying to figure out how not to go back home to Massachusetts for break. I played with the idea of Newport Beach, California, or anywhere warm that was not home, until the day I visited the Outdoor Recreation Program's bulletin board. I was a member of the program and had helped two other fellows lead a backpacking trip for twenty-one students up into the Grand Tetons in Wyoming the previous October. I thought I might find a high adventure trip to use as an excuse to stay out west.

My folks had wanted me home in March but had come around to accepting my backpacking adventures. As a kid, I had grown up with my sister playing in the woodlands behind our house, and as a Boy Scout I had learned the wilderness and leadership skills that I needed when backpacking above the tree line. They had, over time, come to expect that at the drop of a rag wool hat I would head into the mountains of New England to backpack for days or weeks at a time, and that I might even hitchhike to get there and back. I had just turned twenty-one and felt independent and invincible.

I was in luck—tacked on the bulletin board outside the recreation office was a colored flyer that read:

Ice Climbing and Back Country Ski Partner Wanted.

Experience a necessity. Join me for eight days of snow caving in Canada's Mount Assiniboine Providential Park, followed by a day of ice climbing on the world famous Lower Weeping Wall. I am an experienced lead climber. You are experienced in winter camping, backcountry Nordic skiing, and in technical climbing. Call Tim at . . .

I tore off a tab with his name and number and pocketed it. Visiting the Canadian winter wilderness sounded like a good time to me. From his note, Tim seemed organized and seasoned, and I decided to give him a call when I got back to the Men's Co-op a few blocks from campus where I had a room. The co-op was a relatively clean boardinghouse with a big front porch, which was a great place for leaving skis or bicycles without fear of them being stolen.

I shared a room with a theater troupe friend with whom I planned to travel after spring break on a national tour to fourteen western states. That tour would take us over 24,000 miles, to perform in sixty shows with

Montana State University's Theater of Silence, a company of performers who spoke in American Sign Language and annually presented performances to the western deaf community. The fifteen performers in our troupe had been in rehearsal for months, and we were leaving to tour in early April. Originally, I had intended to stay at Montana State only through January and then return to UMass; but after auditioning for this theater troupe and landing a role, with my parents' blessing and encouragement, I had stayed out west.

I called Tim, and he agreed to meet me in the student lounge in the comfy chairs for an interview. Backcountry skiing, backpacking, and technical climbing in the remote Canadian Rockies in the dead of winter was easily twice as dangerous as summer simply because cold weather can kill. Tim had to be sure I could handle it.

While we sat in the student lounge, I told Tim about my backpacking trips and my years on the National Ski Patrol. I was experienced and had the necessary skills, but more than that I wanted Tim to know he could trust me with his life. For his part, Tim told me about his skills in the high country backpacking and climbing on rock and ice.

Tim was an experienced lead climber. This meant that he was skilled at picking the right routes up a rock or ice face and had mastered the techniques of climbing itself—most importantly, placing protection like chocks or ice screws on rock and ice for safety in case of a fall. I enjoyed technical climbing and had been doing it for about three years. I had a natural capacity for it. I liked the mental focus of climbing, the coordination needed, and the physical fitness it required. I climbed everything that looked like it could be climbed.

Tim said that he wanted to spend one of our days in Canada ice climbing. I had never ice climbed before, and had never thought much about it. Tim described the unique equipment involved in ice climbing. It sounded exciting, technical, and dangerous—just perfect for me. Ice climbing would be a new challenge, and I loved challenges, so I said, "Yes, let's go ice climbing and backcountry winter camping."

By the time we'd hashed everything out, we decided that we could trust each other. It was apparent that we could get along with each other, too. The one area where we differed was that I was a spiritual person and Tim was an atheist. We agreed not to talk about religion or God.

We began to plan our trip to spend seven days in Mount Assiniboine Provincial Park backcountry skiing and snow caving, with one day climbing the world-famous Lower Weeping Wall along the Icefields Parkway in Alberta. It would be a ten-day trip overall, including driving time. Tim had the topographic maps we needed, and we pored over them as we planned our skiing route. Over the next few weeks, we gathered our deep winter gear.

Tim owned a lot of the climbing gear that we would use on our trip, including rope, ice screws, nylon webbing, carabiners, crampons, thin line, ice axes, an ice hammer, and ice climbing boots. I did not own any technical climbing gear. I had always rented gear from my outing club at UMass, and I certainly did not own any ice climbing gear. "We'll use my rope, ice screws, carabiners, and webbing to make a harness for you," Tim said. "You'll need to find axes, a hammer, ice climbing boots, and crampons of your own."

As a penniless college student working in the school's food service flipping pancakes, I was unable to afford any more gear beyond my Epoke 900 skis, backcountry Nordic ski boots, gators, and a backpack I had bought in Bozeman using some of my student loan money. I had my gas stove (an Optimus 8R), a sleeping pad, a mess kit, water bottles, a compass, and everything else needed for safe winter camping and wilderness backpacking, except for a deep winter sleeping bag, rated to -30°F. I borrowed one from a generous friend, along with her backpacking shovel for digging out snow caves.

Eventually, I gathered all the gear I needed except for a second ice axe, climbing boots, and crampons, spikes worn on the boots necessary for ice climbing. You cannot ice climb without them. I had rented a pair once before for a backpacking trip in the Grand Tetons where we traversed and went glissading on a glacier, a very fun technique of sliding down a glacier using an ice axe to slow the descent and to stop.

I rented one axe, a hammer, and crampons and so solved most of my equipment problems, or so I thought. I still had to buy, borrow, or rent ice climbing boots. These are specially designed for ice climbing; they are constructed of stiff plastic with insulation to keep your feet warm and have ridged soles that have no flex. They are expensive; a new pair was way beyond my reach. Not having a pair nearly scuttled our trip. "Try finding a used pair of old-time stiff leather alpine ski boots from the sixties," Tim suggested. "They'll be as flat-soled, inflexible, and warm as fancy ice climbing boots." So one snowy afternoon after classes, I walked over to a Bozeman thrift shop where I had purchased wool pants and a wool shirt for our trip. The shop also carried old ski gear. Among the shoes and boots, I found what I was looking for—a pair of old, black leather, buckle-style ski boots in my size. With the boots acquired, that left one last piece of essential equipment: a second ice axe.

In those days, ice axes had straight shafts (today the shafts are more Z-shaped). The shaft is a couple feet long. At the top of the shaft is a serrated bird beak called the pick that, when swung, is used to bite into the ice. The beak sets into the ice and holds there. The shaft, with its spike at the bottom, is then leaned toward the ice so that the spike also sets firmly into the ice. The axe forms a right triangle against the ice wall. Partway up the shaft is usually an O-ring or a hole drilled through the shaft. Through this O-ring or hole a narrow ribbon on nylon webbing is tied in a loop, called the leash. My leash had a bead on it, so that when my hand was through the leash, the bead could be slipped toward my wrist, tightening it. This meant that when the axe was set properly into the ice, I could let go of the shaft and dangle safely by my wrist. It sounds much scarier and more dangerous than it actually is. Also, the leash prevents the possibility of accidentally dropping the axe.

Ice hammers look and function almost exactly like ice axes, except for a few important factors. Ice hammers are smaller, and they have much shorter shafts/handles. The nylon leash is affixed directly to the bottom of the handle instead of the middle. Ice hammers are primarily used to chip at the ice and to use as an ice screwdriver. In the latter function, the hammer is used to spin ice screws into the ice and set them firmly; here, the mechanics are actually more like a wrench than a screwdriver. Ice hammers can also bite into the ice just like ice axes; they can, just like ice axes, be set in such a way that they can support the full weight of a climber. I know this firsthand. The problem with using a hammer instead of an axe is that the climber can never let go of the hammer and dangle on the leash. A person attempting to dangle on a hammer leash causes the bottom of the hammer shaft/handle to pull away from the ice wall, causing the "beak" to release from the ice. I learned this firsthand, too.

Once we had all our gear collected, we packed for our trip. To lighten our loads while backcountry Nordic skiing, we bought expensive freeze-dried food for the week; between us, we carried enough white gas for our stove to last the duration. Our backpacks weighed about twice what we normally carried on our backs for a week walking in the high country since winter backpacking requires additional, heavier gear. In spring, summer, and fall, I carried about thirty-five pounds in my backpack. Our winter packs weighed about seventy pounds each by the time we gathered and packed everything we needed to survive and enjoy the subzero winter weather in Mount Assiniboine Provincial Park, British Columbia. I knew that this would be the most difficult wilderness challenge of my life, and I couldn't wait for it.

☙ 2 ☙

Immortal Youth

Like many families, my family had our share of trouble. I was in Montana to escape it. I'd picked Bozeman because it was far away from Massachusetts and our family crisis, which had dragged on for decades. It started when my sister Andrea was a child, and she accidently hung herself by her cowgirl hat while bouncing on her bed. Our mom had told her not to bounce on the bed, but she did. Our mom was in another room when she heard silence from Andrea's room. Mom dashed in to find her hanging by her neck on the hat string. Andrea had turned blue. They rushed her to the hospital, where the doctors put her in an oxygen tent. Our dad spent the next forty-eight hours in bed with Andrea, holding her in his arms. When she came home from the hospital, she was not the same person. A light had gone out of her eyes. Years went by, and I did not know her any other way than she'd become.

When I was fourteen, on the night of Andrea's high school graduation, she did not come home. Two days later, when she did finally return, having not called, there was a huge scene between her and my parents. The summer continued to be tumultuous. Every dinner was a battlefield. That fall, Andrea went off to the Massachusetts College of Art and Design, but she lasted less than a semester. She had been home about a week when she vanished. Mom was in a panic. She had been talking about her friends in Boston, so Dad took time off from work to see if he could find her.

One day, weeks later, I walked in to find Andrea sitting at the kitchen table. Mom was delousing her hair and boiling her lousy clothes in a pot on the stove. Over dinner, I learned that Dad had seen her in Boston Common with a bunch of hippies. He grabbed her and brought her home. Less than a week after that episode, I got home from school to find the house empty. I expected Andrea to be there and was concerned that she wasn't. My concern shifted to fear when I went to get my backpack and gear out of the attic for an upcoming Boy Scout trip. My pack was gone, along with my sleeping bag and my mess kit.

I knew she'd taken it. I was hurt because in my gut I knew she'd gone, and gone for good. I was angry too, though, because she'd stolen my new pack and my gear and I knew that I could not go camping that weekend, which meant I had to stay home with all the trouble and tension that was simmering. It boiled over that night. The next day my dad took off to Boston again, as he did every day for the next few weeks, to try to find her. He never did. It broke our mother's heart and spirit, too. The ensuing years brought tears upon tears, as the silence deepened and the brokenheartedness reached a devastating level. Each Christmas, we would get a postcard with no return address, so we knew she was alive. Each night our mom would stand alone in the dark of the dining room, holding the curtain back with one hand, staring down Church Street, quietly crying and watching for her prodigal daughter's return.

My senior year in high school, around the time I turned eighteen, in February, Andrea returned with a two-year-old baby in her arms. Our parents welcomed her back, set her up in her own apartment, and found her a job at the public library. I visited the two of them every day after school, for a month, until the day I went to her apartment and found a note on the counter. Andrea said that she was hitchhiking with the baby to the annual Rainbow Family Gathering, which was being held in Virginia that year. It was snowing the day she left. If Andrea's running away the first time broke our mother's heart, her leaving the second time, with a grandbaby on a snowy Saint Patrick's Day, drove our loving mom to a near nervous collapse.

The next year, Andrea was arrested in Oregon for neglect of her three-year-old daughter, Lumeria, and newborn daughter, Ruby. She called home, and our parents paid the bail. The kids were put in foster care. She then fled to Canada. Social services separated the two babies in good homes—one in the East and one in the West. Suffice it to say that during those years my family lived in the deepening pain of estrangement. My home university, the University of Massachusetts Amherst, where I was an English major, was too close to my hometown of Marlborough, where everybody knew us, and where my prominent family struggled to hide our plight in plain sight. Everyone I knew, and everyone who knew us, was respectful of our public silence on the subject of my missing sister. But the last place I wanted to live on earth at that point in my life was anywhere near my family. I needed to escape.

Montana was far, far away from the pain that was my family. The year I spent there was the most terrifying and wonderful year of my life.

In late summer I headed directly into the Montana wilderness, into deep nature that radiates God's Spirit and always, then as now, touches and enlivens my soul, for a month of backpacking with an old friend from England. We met up at Old Faithful at high noon on a certain day inside Yellowstone National Park. Jerry had hitched from Ohio, and I hitched from Bozeman. Together we hitched to trailhead of the high peaks inside Gallatin National Forest. In Bozeman we picked up Richard, and then hitched to the Beartooth Mountains, near Absarokee, Montana, where Jerry broke his ankle a day's hike in. We fashioned him a splint and a crutch and divided his gear between Richard and me and made our way out to the highway to get medical help. Even so, I loved the trip. At Christmas I went home for a brief visit and then quickly fled back to Montana State University for my winter trimester.

As for my sister, my family did not see or hear from Andrea again until I was halfway through my three years at Yale University in the Divinity School. By then, my beautiful and soul-filled sister was married and had been living in Jamaica for seven years. She left her husband and returned to our family home for Christmas that one year, and then she moved to South Beach, Florida, where she lived for many years. I kept in contact with her. Our parents visited with her in Florida. One night in 2007 Andrea fell asleep and went Home to God, God rest her soul, and we rested, too, because her true self rests in God's Love.

⇁ 3 ⇀

Into a Dangerous Foreign Land

That same summer, Tim's dad had given him a new Toyota sedan. And because it was new and a gift from his dad, Tim refused to let me help with the twelve-hour drive from Bozeman through Banff, Alberta, and then on to Mount Assiniboine Provincial Park. His dad had warned him never to let anyone drive his car and not to get a scratch on it, and Tim was adamant about following his dad's rules.

On March Break, just before sunset on the first day of our drive, we pulled into a roadside rest stop to spend the night. We boiled water on our camp stove and ate a freeze-dried dinner, pulled out our sleeping pads and sleeping bags, and slept on top of a couple picnic tables. We awoke in the morning with six inches of fresh powder snow covering us, but we were warm and snug in our sleeping bags.

That morning we left for Mount Assiniboine Provincial Park and arrived around noon. We parked Tim's car on a side road in a small, empty parking lot, strapped on our three-pin skis, hefted our seventy-pound backpacks, and skied across a snow-covered lake, using our compass

Mount Assiniboine with Sunburst Lake. Photograph by
Kurt Stegmüller.

to head toward a log cabin that was clearly marked on our
USGS topographic map.

By dinnertime we had found the *location* of the log
cabin owned by the park, but strangely we could not find
the cabin itself. The long shadows from the tall mountains
around us cast a darkness hours before sunset. We knew
time was limited and hunted for the cabin for an hour or
more. When we could not find it, we skied back to the
lake edge—about a hundred yards away—and using our
compass skills, we triangulated our position using three
mountain peaks within view that corresponded to three
mountain peaks on our map. We were where we were
supposed to be.

We figured out and verified the exact spot where
the cabin should have been according to the map and
skied back to that spot. The cabin was not there. We
were frustrated and nervous. We had not brought a tent
with us. Back in Bozeman, we had carefully researched

and mapped our ski route, noting cabins and places to dig snow caves along the way. We'd intentionally not brought a large and heavy tent which, if we were to divide the weight equally, would have added about four pounds each to our already seventy-pound packs. Thus, the tent was in Tim's car, some ten or more miles across the lake.

Darkness was falling. We were on the windward side of the lake, so the snow was not deep on our side—meaning we would not find snow deep enough to dig a snow cave. Tim hunted for snowdrift anyway as I continued to hunt for the cabin. As we skied around the area, my ski got caught under something. At first, I assumed it was a downed tree branch. I backed off to free my ski and then dug around in the snow to find that my ski had been hooked under the charred remains of a cabin log. I called Tim over, and together we dug around until we discovered that the cabin had burned to the ground, literally only two logs high.

This was bad news. It gets very dark in the forest very quickly, especially among the mountains, and as the evening shadows lengthen, the air cools rapidly. Here it was, the first day of our adventure, and we were already in trouble. It was too far to ski back to the car, and even if we did get across the lake in the subzero cold that we knew was coming, we would never find the car in the dark. Death on our first night out became a possibility.

Again, we talked about heading back to the car, but the car was too far away and we were too exhausted from the long ski across the lake to make it back there. Our only choice was to ski along to the edge of the lake to see if we could find some kind of natural shelter.

The sun had already sunk behind the mountain peaks when, along the bank of the lake, we spotted a frozen water seep that had created an ice flow slab overhanging the lake. The ice made a small sort of cave—or, rather, the roof of what *could* be a cave if we could build walls of snow and ice around it. Under the ice flow, there was just enough room for both of us to lie down side by side with our noses just about touching the ice flow above us. It was a tight squeeze.

I have never really liked being in caves or tight spaces, but it would have to do for the night. We were happy we found possible shelter, but the clock was ticking; night was falling quickly, we were hungry, and it was getting colder by the minute. The wind was blowing on the lake, too, making the air feel even chillier. We had to act quickly to close off the open sides so we could create a warm and safe shelter. Using our shovels and our mittened hands, we cut and broke ice chunks from along the shoreline until we had enough large and thick pieces of ice and snow. These we placed like blocks alongside the flow, leaving one side open so that we could crawl inside.

The experience was quite the way to get to know and trust Tim. We both kept our heads, remained calm, and worked together with near-silent efficiency. I learned then and there that Tim was one to keep his cool in an emergency situation—and Tim learned the same about me. We bonded that night. Little did we know that the day's lesson—learning to trust that the other would stay calm in a life-threatening situation—would be key to our survival on our upcoming ice climb. Surviving in the winter backcountry takes skill, knowledge, the right equipment, and a huge trust in your partner, because your life can and will depend upon him or her. Being in the wilderness is dangerous enough. Being in the wilderness in deep winter is doubly dangerous. I silently thanked God that I was with Tim.

The author's remaining gear from 1980: aluminum gas can, green Polartec booties, plastic honey bottle, compass, blue gator, Epoke skis, and Kletterwerks backpack. Photograph by Peter Panagore.

Once we got the shelter closed off, we fired up our stove, melted ice to a boil, and "cooked" our freeze-dried dinner just before complete darkness fell. Using our flashlights, we hung our packs on trees, unrolled our sleeping pads and tucked them into our ice shelter, then unstuffed our sleeping bags and pulled them up over our bodies as if they were pants. We wriggled, like worms, feet first into the opening we'd left in our makeshift shelter.

Neither of us slept much that night. Mostly, we just tried to rest, uncomfortable but warm and safe, as tightly packed as sardines in a can, with the cold outside and the noise of the ice flow crackling above us. All night long, the lake boomed and shuddered as the temperature dropped and the lake froze ever deeper. The ice flow above us, touching my nose at times, also cracked and shifted around us. Our shelter was claustrophobic. It was disconcerting. I kept thinking, throughout the night, that the thick and heavy flow might crack off at any moment and pin us in our sleeping bags, where we would be found in a week's time or longer, frozen to death. I had never thought about freezing to death before, but I thought about it all that night—about the possibility of being crushed in place and then frozen. I believed I would feel pain if the ice were to pin us, but I also wondered if freezing to death would be as peaceful as it is portrayed in the movies.

Heaven Is Beautiful

4

In the Morning

Yet, we were warm and safe when the sun rose the next morning. And our spirits rose with it, renewed in equal parts by the stunning beauty around us in the morning light as well as by our clever, lifesaving use of a found shelter to survive the night.

The next several days were glorious. We skied many miles into the park and didn't see anybody else the entire time. We dug and lived in a luxurious snow cave for two nights on the way out, and two nights on the way back—it had beds, shelving, a "kitchen," a chimney, comfortable seating, and a heater (a burning candle). Everything except our heater was carved by hand from snow. It got so warm inside our one-room snow cave that we could strip down to our long underwear.

Farther along into the park, we also spent two nights in a log cabin that was marked on our topographic map. In the cabin we found bunk beds, thin mattresses, a woodstove, plenty of wood, and a supply of canned food. We celebrated our comfort and warmth by eating one can of beans.

On our sixth day of having a great time, after our last two nights in our luxury snow cave, we skied out and back toward Tim's car. Throughout the entire ski trip, the snow on the ground was about ten feet deep. Whenever we moved about, we had to keep our skis on. If I were ever to do it again, I think I would bring along snowshoes, too.

When we got back to the lake, the wind was blowing hard against our backs. There was not much snow on the lake, so we took out our ground tarps, tied the tarps to our ski poles with string, and *sailed* over the ice on our skis, back to Tim's Toyota. It was terrific fun to ski-sail on ice! We laughed most of the way.

That afternoon, once we reached the car and stowed our gear, we drove north to lovely Jasper, Alberta, to get a hot and fresh meal at a diner and to buy more food. It was the day before our ice climb on Lower Weeping Wall.

After stocking up on provisions, we left Jasper, driving south on Icefields Parkway, Route 93, and stopping at a park ranger's cabin just a few miles north of our climb. A local in Jasper had mentioned that there might be bunks available there. So, we knocked on the ranger's door and asked if he could give us bunks for the night. He could and kindly did. I think we may have cooked him dinner to thank him before heading to bed.

The next morning we signed into the ranger's logbook as he suggested, indicating that we were going to climb Lower Weeping Wall, a famous ice climb in Banff National Park. People from all over the world go there to climb. Not being an ice climber, I had never heard of it until Tim told me about it, assuring me it was really, really amazing, which it turned out to be.

Signing the logbook allowed us to enter the wilderness area where the Weeping Wall was located. Anytime hikers, backpackers, or climbers enter a wilderness area, they are supposed to sign in, indicate where they intend to go, for how long, and then, upon leaving, sign out. That way the officials can keep track of how many people are in an area so as to control overcrowding and people's safety. It is easy to get lost or injured in wilderness areas; they can be as dangerous as they are beautiful. If someone does not return from the wilderness on or near the day indicated, a search party will be mounted.

❧ 5 ❧

Lower Weeping Wall

Lower Weeping Wall is on the eastern side off the highway, about a hundred yards in. There was a small parking area directly across the highway from the climb. It was not too far from the Columbia Icefield, either, in the middle of that vast Canadian wilderness. Unlike the American Rocky Mountains I have seen, the Canadian Rockies rise pretty much vertically. They're comparatively geologically young; and as such, they are very high mountains that have not been eroded to the extent of the American Rockies.

Lower Weeping Wall lies on the side of Cirrus Mountain, which rises to nearly 11,000 feet about sea level. The ice climb itself was about 450 feet up, or about 45 stories tall; it is considered a water ice grade 4 or WI4, meaning that the climb is nearly vertical for thirty-two feet at a stretch, requiring continuous, exhausting climbing, along with placement of ice screws into the ice for protection. That equates to quite the climb for a first-time ice climber, but I was game, fit, and, like most young people, I believed in my own immortality and invincibility.

We were the last team to arrive at the wall that morning. By the time we hiked in on the tramped-down snow path, there were four or five other climbing teams—amounting to maybe twenty persons—already on the ice and climbing above us. We stopped and dropped our gear to watch the teams climb on the blue and white ice. The ice was beautiful: it looked like a waterfall had been flowing and then instantly froze in place. Tim took a minute to point out the abundance of blue ice on the ice flow. Blue ice, he explained, is hard ice and the best ice for climbing. We were going to have a great day, and we both chatted excitedly as we prepared for our climb.

Within about ten minutes of our arrival, a lead climber on one of the teams screamed as he fell. I'd been watching him lead up on the ice. Being first, he was the one who had climbed the highest, and he moved with a deliberate dexterity. I heard him before I saw him. He must have dropped about fifteen or twenty feet, right down past the last ice screw that he'd placed for his own protection. He had been about 100 feet up on his climb when he fell, plummeting straight down as he screamed. I had been fixing my gear when I heard him and looked up. He was on his rope, and "on belay" (meaning his partner had tight control of his climbing rope). The lead climber bounced a few times at the end of his rope, then smacked hard against the ice wall.

Nobody moved. We all held our breath as he dangled there, watching for signs of life. I felt a jolt of adrenaline course through my blood and tasted metal on my tongue. I was sure that every climber there felt that same surge and tasted that same taste, all of us prepared to spring into action.

Then, he moved . . . and righted himself. I think we collectively exhaled the breath we'd been holding as he waved his arms and shouted, "I'm okay." He had not dropped his axes. After a moment, he set his right axe, then his left, and then he kicked the toes of his crampons into the ice and stood there. We all whooped and cheered.

It had given us all a fright, the climber most of all, no doubt. For a minute I'd thought that our climb might be done before it began. My mood had shifted from joy to seriousness. I felt that everybody there had experienced that same shift, too.

As he continued his climb, we watched him ascend to the last screw he'd placed—the screw that had saved his life. He paused there and, using his ice hammer as a tool, tugged on that screw to make sure it was still secure. Satisfied, he continued his climb.

Tim and I watched him set his next screw and heard the lead climber shout, "Off belay!" His partner returned the call, shouting, "Off belay." Next, his partner shouted, "On belay," and the lead climber returned the call: "On belay." This meant that the lead climber was stopping in order to allow his partner to climb up. In other words, the partner was no longer holding the rope to protect the leader; the leader was now protecting the partner.

And so it is in ice climbing, with each holding the life of the other literally in his or her hands. Tim and I rested a bit to allow the adrenaline rush to subside. Watching that climber fall had made me nervous, and I tried to calm myself with a few minutes of meditation.

Tim was our lead climber; and it was his responsibility to carry all the ice screws up the ice face and place them appropriately and at the proper distance from one another—as protection against falling. Tim had trained as an ice climb leader with professionals, but this was his first solo ice lead. All lead ice climbers need superior skills.

There are subtle nuances to properly placing ice screws. A lead climber must pay attention to ice shatter as the screw is placed, and must "clean" the ice below the screw to ensure that the gate of the carabiners clipped to the screw does not open and allow the rope to escape.

Ice screws are surprisingly small, ranging in size from 10 cm to about 23 cm. In my day, they were placed into the ice at about a 10-degree angle, nearly horizontal. In the years since, after experimentation, it was discovered that a slight upward angle has proven to be a stronger and more secure setting. As the partner, it was my job to clean up the ice screws behind Tim by unscrewing them and carrying them clipped and dangling from my tool belt, in the same way that Tim was carrying them to set them. It is one of the sounds of climbing: ice screws, 'biners, draws, and such jingle together when carried. Tim used his hammer to screw the ice screws into the ice, while I used my hammer to unscrew each one later.

As we prepared to climb, I chose to use my one ice axe in my left hand and an ice hammer in my right hand. It seemed like a workable idea at the time. As it turned out, it was an ignorant choice on my part, maybe the worst choice I've ever made in my life.

Having checked our gear and finding that everything was in order, we wrapped long lengths of blue webbing around our legs and waists to create our harnesses, the webbing tied neatly and securely in square knots. We each picked a locking carabiner and attached it to our harness. Our lives depended on that carabiner and harness. We checked each other's harness and carabiner by tugging on them, just to make sure everything was done correctly. Next, we strapped on our crampons. Tim clipped on his collection of ice screws, carabiners, and slings (webbing lengths individually tied together in square knots). I slung my hammer on its sling over my shoulder, and picked up our coiled rope. Tim had his two axes, and I carried my one axe and my climbing hammer. The sun was shining. It was warm enough for a March day. We were excited, yet a bit trepidatious at the onset of our adventure, and very, very focused.

At the very bottom of the climb, Tim said, "I'm putting my life in your hands. I trust you." I replied in kind, and we began our ascent. Tim approached the ice, stopped, and looked over at me as I stood a few feet behind. He looked up the ice wall and then shouted, "On belay." I replied, "On belay." We were off.

The looped end of our doubled rope was tied in a bow-line knot to his locking carabiner clipped to his harness. The bitter (or free) ends of our doubled rope were tied as one knot to my locking carabiner, which was clipped to my harness. As Tim was the lead, our rope was wrapped around my waist. I also held the rope in my right and left mittened hands, paying out the rope slowly while keeping a bit of tension on the line as Tim climbed up, setting the first swing of his right ice axe.

He climbed with ease and concentration, making sure that each swing of his axe bit securely into the ice, and that with each setting of the crampons on his feet his footing was secure. At about fifteen feet up, Tim stopped. It was time to place our first protective ice screw. I watched as he searched the ice just above him for a good place to set his left ice axe, then set and anchored it firmly and securely. No climber wants to burn out his or her calves, so Tim reached down with his right axe and chopped a step into the ice for his right foot; this way, he could stand more comfortably.

Now, he had to pick where to place his first screw. He chose a spot in the ice near his waist area on his right-hand side because it was easier to apply pressure with his arm. Tim cleaned the ice by chipping the bad (softer) ice away from the good (harder) ice underneath. Next, he chipped a starter hole in the ice, chipping in the same spot until he created a divot, and then he grabbed one of his screws from the harness rack hanging at his waist, put its end on the ice, pressed in, and turned it by hand. The screw bit into the ice. He grabbed the screw again and very carefully twisted it while pushing in. When he could not screw it in any farther, he used his ice axe as a wrench, turning the screw in the rest of the way, setting it almost firmly in place. A bumpy piece in the surface of the ice stopped him from turning the screw just that little bit more it needed, so he chipped it away, cleaned the ice a little extra, and then finished setting the screw securely using his axe as his wrench.

"Placing ice screws as protection is the hardest part about climbing ice," Tim had told me. Watching him above me, I started to believe it. He unclipped one the carabiners from his waist. It had a sling of webbing clipped into it, with a second carabiner at the other end. The first carabiner was clipped into the ice screw, and the second was clipped over our rope. Tim tugged the rope against the screw. Feeling good about it, he continued up as I waited below and payed out the line. At about fifteen feet above his first ice screw, Tim stopped and set another ice screw for protection. He stopped, and shouted, "Off belay." I replied, "Off belay."

I approached the ice wall and shouted, "On belay." Tim replied, "On belay." He tensioned the rope. I looked up and saw Tim and the other climbing teams. I took a breath to focus my head, and began the first and last ice climb of my life.

I started the day fresh and strong and began my climb with care, focus, and strength. When I reached the first ice screw Tim had placed, I stopped, unscrewed it from the ice, clipped it to my harness, and unclipped it from our rope. All the way up the 450-foot climb, for the entire day, we repeated this series of moves. Tim would climb and set the screws, and I would follow and remove the screws, with all the aluminum clinking and clanking from our harnesses.

By mid-morning, my right arm was exhausted because I could not rest it by hanging from the leash on my ice hammer. The muscles of my right arm would continue screaming for the rest of our climb, severely slowing our ascent. Unlike all the other climbers on the face that day, I had to stop frequently, and for longer and longer periods, to rest my right arm. You may think that I could have switched the hammer to my left arm and the ice axe to my right arm, right? Yes, I thought of that. I thought a lot about that . . . and I wished I could have done so. But that was impossible to do without falling.

Let me explain.

❦ 6 ❧

Just a Day Climb

When climbing, one needs to keep three points of contact at all times—two feet, and one hand, or two hands and one foot (or ice axes, as the case may be); otherwise, the climber is either dangling from two arms, or falling. Yes, one can hold on with one hand, but that takes an enormous amount of strength; and if one does do that, he or she does so only for a brief time. All of this meant that I could not switch the axe to my right hand and the ice hammer to my left. Maybe the maneuver is possible by someone far more skilled than I was, but, for the life of me, I couldn't figure out how to make the switch without falling. The hammer was in my right hand, and that was that.

As much as I wanted to switch the axe for the hammer—and I wanted it a lot—I couldn't do it. I had to hang on to that hammer with all my might every time I used it, and I used it all the time unless I was letting it dangle to rest my arm. Our climb was much, much slower by several hours than it would've been if I had been climbing with two axes. With only one, I was able to climb a little ways, then had to rest. I would climb a little more, then rest again. That's how it went all day.

Tim was anxious, as was I, because the sun was crossing the sky and we knew that every minute of delay increased the likelihood that we might end our ascent in the dark, and that would be bad. Toward the end of the day, totally exhausted because of my arm, I looked on with Tim as all the other teams completed their climbs above us and then rappelled down the three pitches of 150 feet each.

Ice climbing can be a wet sport, and I learned it the hard way that day. Whenever Tim cleaned the ice to set a screw, or chop a foothold for himself, he'd shout, "Ice!" and that ice would fall directly on or near me. It often hit me or my helmet and frequently went down the neck of my jacket, and down my back. We perspired a lot, too, of course—or at least I did.

As we climbed into the afternoon, we ate the food that we carried in our pockets for lunch and had snacks to keep our energy up. I carried my two plastic water bottles that I used for backpacking. One was quart-sized, the other a quart and a half. I drank through those carefully, measuring my water intake against my sweat outflow. Occasionally, I would pop a piece of ice into my mouth, as much to cool me down as to give me drink. We'd planned to carry enough food and water to get us to the top, since rappelling down was so quick and easy; we figured we would be down by late afternoon, and cooking dinner beside our tent well before sunset. Instead we reached the top near sunset. By the time we reached our last pitch up, I was wet to the skin, cold, and not too happy.

It was just a day climb. That is what the guidebooks say. That is what all the other climbers planned for: a day. We planned for the same, and carried only what we needed for a day climb and nothing more. We did not carry a stove or gas, or food for dinner, or sleeping bags, or any extra or extraneous gear—not even extra water or food. Nobody did. We traveled light on purpose, just like everybody else. You might guess that I've thought a lot about the mistakes we made that day . . . and I have. I attribute it to the exuberance and optimism of my youth and my false belief in my own invulnerability and immortality. In hindsight, of course, I was foolish to believe I was strong enough to climb all that way with a hammer— and I was ignorant of the hazard that choice would cause.

Meanwhile, after many hours of slow but methodical climbing, we reached the top of our climb, about 450 feet up. A climb that should have taken seven hours or less instead took us around twelve hours to complete. I say "around" because, for one, I was not wearing a watch, and, for two, my mind was focused the entire time on my task and my body, not on the passage of time . . . other than to know that time was passing, and that in passing, our situation was becoming more dangerous by the minute.

Climbing is intensely physical, but it also requires constant mental focus. This is what I enjoyed most about it: the only thing that matters when you're climbing is climbing; the rest of life completely fades away. I couldn't focus on the height, or the danger, or the fear. The fear was there for me every time I climbed, but the mastery of that fear is what made me feel alive. When climbing, there was only me—where I was, in that spot, on whatever face I was climbing. Nothing else existed except for my climbing partner and me. Here, there was nothing else to care about, think about, or consider—nothing else mattered but the task at hand. Every move must be efficient, clean, and thought through. No energy is wasted; no move is clumsy or without purpose.

When climbing, there were no concerns, no worries, no love life, no home life, no anything other than the climb itself. If my mind wandered from the task at hand or the place I was, I was putting not only my life but also my climbing partner's life in danger. Focus, focus, focus, master fear, pay attention, think only of my position at the moment and my next move—that was the name of the game.

The last section of our climb was to the small ledge on which Tim sat waiting for me, anchored into the ice by screws. The ledge was an ice-covered rock about four times the size of a twelve-seat dining table. As I crawled up over the edge, eager to rest for the first time since early that morning, I took in the view.

It was amazing. The Columbia Icefield was visible in the distance. The ice was gorgeous. But the sun was setting, and the temperature had begun to drop steeply, quickly, and steadily. Now at rest, I realized my clothes were soaked; I was wet to the skin from sweat and the ice falling down my shirt, melting against my skin. Tim was wet, too. We were very cold, but not as cold as we knew we were about to be.

❧ 7 ❧

Alone and Cold

We began to shiver as we watched the last of the other climbing teams reach the bottom of their rappels below. We watched as the last team of three walked back to the parking lot, carrying their gear. One guy in the last team looked up at us and waved his arms. We waved back. He waved again.

We were alone, Tim and I, high on the ice mountain in the middle of a vast and empty wilderness. A feeling of foreboding overtook me, but I fought it off just as I'd fought off all of my fears all day. We were in trouble, and we knew it. It was obvious. Neither of us carried a watch, so we didn't know what time it was; but as we watched the sun set behind the distant mountain peaks to the west, we knew we had to talk about what to do and make choices soon. We remained levelheaded, but we were out of food and water, and we didn't have anything to save our lives except our wits, skills, determination, and each other.

We were not far from the parkway, a portion of which we could see; but this was the borderland of rural eastern British Columbia, and there were no cars on the road that evening. As we sat on the ledge with our legs hanging over the side, our shivering got worse. My teeth chattered, or more accurately, clattered. My jaw was just about out of my control. The noise of my teeth hitting my teeth made me think about my skull, my skeleton, my bones, my muscles that twitched all on their own, and about how fragile the human body is.

Where was the line, I thought, between my conscious mind that controlled my thoughts and movements, and the actions of my body, which suddenly seemed to have a mind of its own, making me twitch and shake, clatter and shiver. I fought to keep control. "Shivering is good because it's the body's way of producing heat," Tim told me. He was right, of course, but my chattering teeth made it difficult to talk. Tim was shivering, too, his teeth chattering.

We had not planned on spending the night up there, but we also knew that we had to consider it as an option. We were in a dangerous situation that could turn deadly. We were exposed, vulnerable, and determined not to die.

Earlier that winter, while volunteering on the National Ski Patrol, I had forced numerous skiers off of the mountain at Bridger Bowl ski resort in Bozeman because of frostbite and potential exposure during a -50°F week. That winter I had studied up on hypothermia and frostbite, so it was still fresh in my mind. Tim's and my shivers were the beginning stage of what I knew quickly could and probably soon enough would turn into hypothermic risk of death from exposure to the cold. I told Tim what I knew and about the possible stages of hypothermia. We both needed to know what its process was so we could keep an eye on each other.

Here's what happens in hypothermia: Shivering begins, and then violent shivering. The physiological responses of the body are geared to preserve heat; we're geared to survive. Hypoglycemia, or low blood sugar, may present itself as cells decrease their consumption of glucose.

Micromuscular miscoordination comes next—movements become slow and labored, accompanied by stumbling and mild confusion. Surface blood vessels contract as the body focuses its remaining resources on keeping the vital organs warm, and the skin becomes pale and sometimes blue. As body temperature decreases, further physiological systems falter; heart rate, respiratory rate, and blood pressure all decrease. Difficulty speaking, sluggish thinking, and amnesia start to appear, and a lack of coordination and stumbling are also usually present. Cellular metabolic processes shut down.

Below 86°F, exposed skin becomes blue and puffy, muscle coordination becomes very poor, walking becomes almost impossible, and the person exhibits incoherent/irrational behavior or can even go into a stupor. The pulse and respiration rates decrease significantly, but fast heart rates can occur. Major organs may fail, but because of decreased cellular activity in stage 3 hypothermia, the body will actually take longer to undergo brain death. Lastly, one falls asleep.

There is a thing called "paradoxical undressing" that occurs in up to 50 percent of hypothermia cases. The person becomes confused and begins to disrobe because he or she feels hot, which of course increases the rate of heat loss. Wikipedia says "one explanation for the effect is a cold-induced malfunction of the hypothalamus, the part of the brain that regulates body temperature. Another explanation is that the muscles contracting peripheral blood vessels become exhausted . . . and relaxed, leading to a sudden surge of blood (and heat) to the extremities, fooling the person into feeling overheated." In my case, it felt as if my core was suddenly superheated.

Only some of this had occurred so far. We sat there shivering, discussing what to do while watching the sky go dark as the stars came out. We had a choice: We could spend the night where we were and snuggle into the mountain as best we could, or we could try to get off that mountain, and fast.

If we stayed put, rescuers would find us in the morning. One of the first rules of wilderness survival is if you get lost, stay put. We had signed the logbook at the ranger's station. The climber from the last team had seen us at the top and waved as he was leaving. We were not lost, but staying put might be the best choice, if we could survive the night. In the warmth of the morning, in the daylight, we could rappel.

On the back side of the ice ledge was a vertical wall. I think it was stone, not ice. I got up to look it over. It was about ten feet from the ledge. If we could tuck our bodies against the mountain and spoon together for warmth, that might save our lives—but we were already so cold that, even together, we thought we might not produce enough body heat between us.

The way I imagined it was with Tim against the rock face with my nose to his helmeted head, snuggled against his back for warmth with my back exposed to the weather. It did not have to be me on the outside, but that is the way I came to think that whoever was on the outside likely would die, and surely the other one might, too. We had been in the mountains for more than a week, so we knew how cold it was going to be that night.

There were no clouds in the sky. That was both good and bad. It was bad because that meant that all the heat of the day, baked into the earth by the sun—though there had been little heat that sunny day—would rise and escape into the atmosphere. If there had been clouds there would have been a thermal inversion, whereby the clouds act as a sky blanket, forcing the heat to stay closer to the ground.

There was no thermal blanket of clouds overhead, but there were thousands of stars. This was the good news. We knew that it was going to be dangerous to try to escape our situation by moving around on the cliffside in the dark. We could slip and fall off. We might stumble and break a bone. We could get lost, although that was unlikely. But with thousands of stars coming out overhead, there might be just enough light to move about. It was very dangerous to stay still, maybe more dangerous than moving about. Just sitting there and talking was starting to kill us.

We decided that if we spent the night tucked up against the mountain at the back of the ledge, using each other's bodies for warmth, we were probably going to die—and if we were probably going to die by spending the night, then we'd be better off dying while trying to get down off the mountain. So, that's what we decided to do.

I was already in worse shape than Tim. My body had begun to shiver violently and uncontrollably. It was a scary feeling. I learned that night that courage is not feeling "no fear"; courage is feeling fear and moving forward bravely anyway. We were both scared, although to keep up morale neither of us talked about it. There was no point. We knew each other very well by this time. We each knew the other was afraid, but we also knew that together we were courageous, capable, and trustworthy.

⮘ 8 ⮚

Galaxies for Light

It is sobering to see one's own death nearby. It bonds people together when you know that your very survival, your heartbeat, sits in combined hands, and in the will and determination of you and your partner. Our week in the winter wilderness had taught me that Tim had a level and a rational head. He never panicked. As it turned out, neither do I. We believed in each other. We had to. And, by believing in each other, we found the strength to believe in ourselves. We were fighters. We were a team. We aimed to get off that mountain and to survive. We were embarking on what we knew was going to be the longest night of our lives.

As we sat on the cliff talking about our choice to push on, Tim was pulling up our 300-foot rope as quickly as he could. Because it was getting dark, and because we were in a desperate hurry, Tim forgot to lay the line neatly and correctly, which resulted in a 300-foot tangled knot.

More stars came out, making it easier to see. There must have been a million stars overhead, no exaggeration. When you get far enough away from light pollution, you can see every color of every visible star in the sky—red, yellow, blue, white, and orange. On that cliff we could see millions of stars and galaxies of every color. The sky was a blanket of bright twinkling lights. It was not pitch-black where we sat, as it would have been if it had been a cloudy night. If it were pitch-black out, we would have had to stay put; but because there were so many stars in the sky, they actually provided some light by which to see. We had options. Not a lot of light, but just enough.

My eyes are very light sensitive—so much so that I must wear sunglasses or a hat when I'm outside even on cloudy days. The flip side of this is that I can see pretty well in very low light, and I could see the details of the rope better than Tim could. I was then and remain today a rope man. Rope, knots, bends, lashings, and whippings have always come easily to me. Thus, it was my job to untangle our rope. But rope handling is tactile, and I needed to feel it as much as see it to succeed. This meant that I had to take off my mittens. Untangling the 300-foot knot took what felt like hours. I don't know how long it actually took, but it was long enough to set frostbite into all of my fingertips, in particular three of them on my right hand.

Ever since that night, I must wear gloves whenever the temperature falls below fifty degrees. At forty-nine degrees my fingertips ache; in colder temperatures, they tend to dry and crack and bleed. I've also discovered over the course of my lifetime that frostbite is cumulative; since that night, whenever my fingers get just a little too cold in the wintertime, the frost damage increases.

All that night, as Tim and I sat on the ledge making choices, frostnip bit into our fingertips, and the tips of our toes and noses, and on our cheeks and earlobes. As we sat there and I worked the rope, my shivering continued to increase in violence. My body was spastic, bouncing up and down, and difficult to control, making it increasingly difficult to make my hands and arms do what I wanted them to do in order to untangle the rope.

Tim, who was not in as bad of shape due to the cold as I was, kept telling me in a calm and caring voice that my shivers were a good sign, because they meant my body was trying to keep itself warm. He was right. Hearing him say it gave me heart. I think at one point he even put his hand on my shoulder as he said it. Tim is a good guy.

We sat there side by side as I untied the knots and pulled the long line through itself, always being extra careful not to drop the rope over the edge. I could not tie one end to myself until I got close to the end of my task: to untie the rope, I had to work from both ends. This made my job easier and faster, but it also increased the risk of losing the entire line over the side. I never let the rope dangle down, as I might have done during daylight, or if I could've tied one end to myself. That meant I had to be particularly careful to lay the line safely and correctly every time I untangled or untied a section.

Tim was mostly silent while I concentrated on the line. At one point, he said, "The moon is going to rise, and when it does, we'll have more light to move about with added safety." In any case, we had to wait for the moon to rise because even though I could see pretty well in low light, Tim could not. The starlight was just not bright enough of a light source for us to be able to stand and walk safely.

Eventually, I untangled the entire line. My violent shivers and chattering teeth lasted for hours. I'm pretty sure that by the time I finished untangling and setting the rope, Tim had the violent shivers, too.

As Tim had predicted, a near three-quarter moon rose over the mountain ridge, casting a lot more light. Suddenly, we could see just about everything there was to see. We could almost see the colors of our clothing and could definitely see the valley below us, the mountains around us, the Columbia Icefield to the west—and, most importantly, the details of the mountain where we sat. I had never been so glad to see the moon in all my life. There was enough light to push on, thank God.

Tim was a rationalist, a humanist, and an atheist . . . or at least an agnostic who leaned heavily to atheism. He tolerated my faith in God, and I tolerated his lack of it. It didn't really matter all that much since we liked each other. (In the years since that day, as it turns out, quite a number of my friends are atheists. They tell me that I'm nuts, and I tell them that they'll find out who was nuts the day they die. Then, we laugh about it!) Early on, Tim and I had agreed to disagree and leave God off the table of our conversation topics. I was not the type then, nor am I now, to make it a personal mission to convert anybody. I prayed a lot that night. I did not ask to be rescued; I asked that God be present to me, and to us, as we struggled for our survival.

I coiled our rope and we stood up, staying back from the cliff's edge. Standing was difficult because our muscles were sore, tired, stiff, and beginning to malfunction because of the cold. Tim said that we had better tie ourselves together in case one of us fell, so the other might be able to save him. I took off my mittens again, uncoiled a portion of the rope—maybe twelve feet worth—and tied the rope to itself, leaving the twelve feet loose and handing the coil to Tim. He slung the coil over his shoulder, tied a bowline knot close to the coil, and then clipped the bowline to his harness carabiner. I took my end of the of the rope and tied my bowline there and clipped that to my harness carabiner. We both felt safer knowing that we might be able to save the life of the other if one of us fell . . . or perhaps that we would die together if one went over and the other could not stop his fall.

~ 9 ~

First Rappel

Tim led and I followed as we carefully traversed the narrow trail along the face to the first rappel point. The mountain face was to our right, and we could touch it with our hands, or bump against it with our shoulders. Immediately to the left of the trail was our 450-foot drop. Each step of the way was carefully placed. We moved slowly, in part out of caution, in part out of necessity due to the worsening condition of our bodies and minds. Tim had a pretty good idea where the first and nearest rappel was, because while he was waiting for me to complete my slow ascent he had had time to watch the other climbers descend. I myself had no idea where it was or what to expect. Tim said he knew where it was, and that was good enough for me. The trail was stony, icy, and snow covered. We spoke little and only as necessary: We'd already learned that it was important to conserve what little strength we had left, and speaking took too much energy.

Looking down by hanging over the edge from where we stood, we could see the landing area in the moonlight.

It was white because of the snow cover and surrounded by darkness. At the bottom of the rappel was a large, flat, and irregularly shaped landing area covered in knee-deep snow. The landing area was about twenty-five feet wide and close to the mountain. It projected out roughly the same distance, but narrowed at its cliff edge to about ten feet wide. The exertion of our walk on our traverse had warmed us up a little, but that warmth was fleeting, and we soon started shivering again.

In front of us was a small conifer tree rooted into the rock, with a trunk about eight inches in diameter. "We'll use the tree for the anchor of our rappel," Tim said. He explained that he had seen the other teams wrap a knotted piece of webbing around the tree and then slip their rope through the loop of webbing. The other teams tossed the two bitter ends of their ropes over the side. They did this instead of wrapping their rope around the tree. When I asked why, Tim said he thought it was to prevent the rope from freezing to the rough bark of the tree. It would be easier to pull the rope down to us if we slipped it through a length of webbing. That made sense, and it was the right way to do it.

If we had been in our right minds—and we were not—that is exactly how we would've done it. Instead, we talked about the cost of webbing. If we did it the way we should have, the way all the other teams had, then Tim would lose that length of webbing. Webbing was expensive for college students. We decided then and there that it was a perfect waste of a perfectly good length of webbing—and, besides, we might need that piece to survive later on. There was no way, given how cold it was and how everything was already frozen, that that rope would stick to the tree. No way. None. It was logical. We decided that we didn't want to leave the webbing behind. We decided we would save it, and instead wrap the rope directly around the tree. It is no surprise in hindsight that it was a stupid choice and one that largely contributed to my death. But Tim was convinced that it would be okay, and I believed him.

We unclipped ourselves from our rope and untied our bowline knots. Tim unslung the coil from his shoulder, laid it down on the snow, and untied the clove hitch that was holding the rope in its coil. He bent over and carefully divided the coil into seemingly equal halves, then opened a short length of line between the two halves. He put one half to the right of the tree, and the other half to the left of the tree. I watched and waited, ready to comment or intervene if necessary. Tim worked silently. He handed me the short length that represented the middle of the entire length of rope as he prepared to toss both coils over the side. My job was to hold my part of the rope to make sure that we did not lose it, because to do so meant certain death. His job was to toss the coils on either side of the tree.

He tossed. I held. It worked. I laid the line against the tree but kept a grip on it just in case. Tim looked over the edge and pulled one side of the line up to even it out as best he could. He could see that the bitter ends lay in the snow like black snakes way below us. I let go of the rope. Tim volunteered to take the risk and go first because he had tossed the line. He pulled the double line up toward him, then threaded and clipped it through his double carabiner rig that created a metal figure eight. Both carabiners were the kind that lock, ensuring that the rope would not accidentally pop out. This figure-eight rig was common enough in those days.

We looked each other in the eye just before he went over the edge. I am sure he was scared to go. I was scared to stay alone. He leaned back against the rope, making it taut, then let it slip through his mittens in a controlled manner as he leaned back and stepped to the very edge of the ledge. We watched each other's eyes. Mine said: *You can do it*. His said: *You, too*. He leaned out over empty space until he was almost parallel to the soles of my boots. Then, he took a step or two down, and I lost sight of him.

I lay down in the snow and inched my way to the edge so I could watch him descend. Tim was dangling in space with his head up and his feet down, sliding down the rope with control and stopping every so often. It only took a few minutes for him to reach the wide ledge below. When he got down there, he looked like a silhouette. I waited until he waved both arms at me—that meant it was my turn.

It was so silent up there. There was no wind. In the distance, I heard a car. I saw that Tim had heard it, too. We both looked out toward the highway and waited as headlights illuminated the roadway. I stood up and backed up against the cliff behind me. When I could see the car, I jumped up and down, waved my arms, and yelled as loudly as I could. I could hear Tim yelling below me, too, and guessed he was doing exactly as I was. But the car drove on; the driver never saw us.

With a bit of despair, I readied myself as Tim had and prepared to go over the edge. I threaded, clipped, and locked the double line into my figure-eight carabiners. I had to take my mittens off to do this. My fingers were stiff and burned with cold.

I had rappelled several times before and liked it. I liked the rush, the pounding of my heart, the focus of my mind, and the knowledge that my life depended on a rope, keeping my head, my skills, and my actions. My previous rappelling experiences had always been with my feet against a cliff, using a technique of walking down the cliffside, with my body perpendicular to the cliff and my back parallel to the ground. This was to be my first rappel in open space. I'd watched Tim make his descent so I might get an idea how to do the same before I started. I told myself that it would be okay, and that the friction created by this figure-eight carabiner rappel would easily control the rate of my descent. Tim had said it would be easy and not to worry, that if he could do it, so could I. And now, it was my turn. I felt fear, but I tamped it down by sheer force of mind, will, and my growing determination simply to survive. Besides, I had no choice. I had to go.

I took up tension in the rope, faced the mountainside, and inched my way back until I felt the edge under my right foot crampon, then stepped back to the edge with my left foot. With both feet now on the edge, I slowly and carefully leaned back out into empty space, moving slightly to the side until the tree was between my feet and the angle of my body made it possible to trust the rope, the tree, my carabiners, and myself. My back was parallel to the ground and my body perpendicular to the mountainside, the opposite of what I was accustomed to doing.

Slowly, I walked myself down, letting the rope slide in a controlled manner through my leather-mittened hands. Once I was over the edge, there was no going back up; I was committed and determined. I continued my descent, watching the ledge disappear from view until my legs no longer reached the ledge. Now, it was my turn to hang on to our rope, my turn to be free and dangling in the air with my feet pointed downward and my head toward the stars. Letting the rope slide through my hands, I stopped on occasion—just to make sure that I could stop—until I reached our landing area and Tim, who was waiting for me, holding the double rope as steadily as he could.

The snow on our landing area was knee deep and soft. I was not going fast, but I sort of landed on top of Tim and knocked him down. I rolled away a bit. Then, we lay there in the snow for a few minutes to rest and gather ourselves for our next task. I watched the stars. There were more stars than I had ever seen in my life, and the sky was so clear. Soon after, Tim struggled to his feet, and I listened as he tried to pull our rope down. I expected that it would be easy and was surprised to hear him muttering and swearing. The swearing itself was not a surprise. We were college students, after all, and I'd spent my summers working in the trades where the same word was frequently used as a noun, verb, adverb, adjective, and even an expletive. What surprised me was that Tim was swearing at that moment.

10

One Way Up

I tried to sit up but could not quite manage it. My muscles were stiff, and so I sort of inadvertently tipped over as I sat up. I went with it and rolled over onto my stomach, pulled my knees in, pushed up on my hands, and worked myself into a standing position, then slowly turned around to see what Tim was doing. He was pulling hard on one length of the rope, and I could see that it was not budging. He called me over.

I took a step. The snow was knee deep and normally would not have been that difficult to move about in, but I found myself teetering like I was an old man or had some kind of muscle disease. Tim watched me.

"You're moving funny," he said.

"I know," I said, "I'm losing coordination." To my ears, his words and my words sounded slurred, as if I was drunk. I sounded drunk. I walked like I was drunk. That was bad. As I walked over to Tim, I lost my balance and fell on my knees. We had to get out of there before the cold killed us, and it was killing us. It was after us, pursuing us, and I thought of it as my enemy.

The moon had begun to rise over the top of the peaks far above us, bringing us lots of light; and for that we were very glad. Tim continued to pull on the rope. He pulled harder and harder, lifting himself using all his weight. He said he thought our rope might have been wet after all and had frozen to the rough bark of the tree 145 feet above us at the cliff peak. That made sense.

I stumbled my way over to Tim. We grabbed the rope together and pulled down on it. Nothing.

We tried again with all our might and weight. Nothing.

We rested, then pulled again, and again, and again. Nothing.

We were desperate and determined, but the rope would not budge. We kept our heads. We had to get the rope loose. It was either get the rope free, or die on that ledge.

The choice was clear and unfortunate: One of us had to climb back up to the tree and free the rope. The problem was that the climb above us was a 145-foot inverted incline. In layman's terms, it was a 145-foot overhang. There was no ice on the overhang. It was all rock, and the entire under-side of the overhang was in dark shadow. There was no way either of us was going to climb that—even if we had the strength, which we did not. Even if it had been daylight, and warm, and summer—which it was not—neither of us had the skills to ascend a 145-foot overhang.

We were stymied and fearful. We both sat down in the snow next to the hanging rope and looked up at the stars and the moon, and off to the valley below us. Tim said he knew how to tie a Prusik hitch, a friction hitch used to ascend climbing rope. I had never heard of it, but Tim said he'd tied the knot before, and had practiced using it a little bit. The Prusik hitch was for an emergency situation, which ours definitely was.

The added trouble for us was that our rope was not fixed to the ground, so there was nothing to tie it to on our end, and up top it was not secure; it was merely frozen in place. Ice, bark, and friction held it fast to the tree, but it was not *tied*. It was actually a loose rope when you think about it, not secured to anything. Tim planned to tie one Prusik hitch to each piece of our double line and climb up. We knew that at any moment, at any place during his climb back up—ten feet above us, or a hundred feet above us—the ice holding the rope to the tree might break loose and Tim could fall to his death.

We talked about it. Tim said that he felt responsible for our situation. It was, he said, his fault that we were there because he was the lead climber; he was the boss, and I was new to ice climbing. I did not blame him, but I thanked him for saying so. Yes, he was the experienced one, but we'd both made choices that had gotten us into this situation.

Tim was a brave man. That much I knew for sure. He was not fearless or reckless—a fearless person has no fear, and a reckless person doesn't take into account danger or the results of risk taking. Tim was courageous and calculating. He was afraid, as was I, that he might fall. But he calculated correctly that unless one of us acted we both would die.

We talked a little about what it would be like to freeze to death, sitting there, looking out at the moonlit landscape, with our eyes open until we died. We talked about what it would be like for the climbers who would certainly find us the next day, and the horror they would feel when they saw our faces and our bodies. We had no other choice: Tim had to climb.

My job was to tie the bottom of the ropes to my body and roll them as tightly as I could into my waist. By doing so, I would try to create as great a tension in the rope from top to bottom as possible, and thus hold the rope as steadily as I could while Tim ascended.

Friction hitches such as a Prusik hitch grab into a rope when a load is applied to it and release the rope when the load is removed. Our Prusik hitch involved looping a thin nylon cord around a rope. Tim cut two long lengths, each maybe eight feet long, of low-stretch 6 mm nylon accessory climbing cord. Climbing cord is very strong. He tied the ends of each length of cord together using a square knot to form two four-foot-long loops.

Tim hitched one loop to one side of the double rope, and the other loop to the second side of our double rope. These loops created two four-foot-long slings for his feet to slip inside of and stand on. "Have you tried these Prusik hitches before, and are you really sure you want to do this?" I asked Tim again. We both knew the answer. Tim repeated, yes, he'd tried this Prusik technique when he had learned how to use it, and yes, he had to climb. With his right foot in the right sling, his left foot in the left sling, and his hands on each Prusik hitch respectively, Tim was ready to begin his ascent 145 feet up the rope to the rough-bark tree. His intent was to reach the peak, peel the frozen rope from the tree, put a sling around the tree, and rappel back down to me. It was an extremely dangerous maneuver. Just before he started, and before I rolled myself into the rope, I stopped him, repeating that we'd gotten ourselves into this situation together, that it was not his fault alone. I shared the burden equally. We hugged.

I started thinking about what I had once heard from another climber: "Once you get above a certain height on a wall, it doesn't matter how high you've climbed because if you fall from thirty feet or three hundred feet or three thousand feet, it will kill you." That climber added, "It's not the fall that kills you anyway; it's the sudden stop at the end." Gallows humor.

I grabbed the rope, wrapped it around myself with one loop, took off my mittens, clumsily tied a double half-hitch, and tightened the rope around my waist. There was not much excess line. I lay down at Tim's feet and rolled and rolled until I got the rope as taut as I could get it. When he was ready, he began to climb right above me. I positioned myself to watch him as best I could.

Tim was already exhausted. We both were. And Tim had to climb unprotected. If he fell, he could die. We kept our heads, but we both knew with every breath we took that the rope could break free at any moment and Tim could fall.

The ropes jerked as Tim started up, by lifting his right foot while sliding his right mittened hand up the rope and pushing the Prusik hitch upward. He put weight on his right foot and pushed down on the Prusik cord with all his might in order to check it. The Prusik hitch held firmly in place because of friction on the rope; he had tied it correctly. "It works," he said.

Tim lifted his left foot while slipping the left Prusik hitch up the rope with his left mittened hand. The rope swayed. He waited a moment to see if the left hitch would also hold fast under his weight. It did. He began to climb, slowly and carefully. Each time he moved one hand and one leg, the rope jerked and swayed. The whole setup was so sloppy, and it swayed with each step no matter how hard I tried to keep the rig steady. I told Tim again that he was brave, and thanked him again, adding that I would do my best to steady the rope. He said nothing and continued his climb.

The higher Tim got, the more the rope swayed and twisted. It was dead silent. I waited below in the cold snow, feeling my body growing colder and more sluggish by the minute. The shivering had stopped for both of us. That was not a good sign, given the circumstances.

Tim climbed up and up, slowly, steadily, with rhythm. He got to twenty or twenty-five feet as I watched from below.

The jerking motion required to shift the hitches, maybe combined with the swaying of the rope, suddenly forced the frozen rope to break loose from the tree.

It happened so quickly. I felt the rope jerk me and unwind a bit. It rolled me a half turn until my face was in the snow. Tim shouted, "FALLING!" I was directly beneath him. He had his crampons on. I braced myself and tried to roll away as quickly as I could, but I was tied in and could not roll far. Tim fell and landed partly on me and partly on the snow. We lay still for a minute. I asked him how he was. He was unbroken and unhurt. "Me too," I said.

The rope was free. It felt like a miracle that it had come free before he had climbed very high up. I kept imagining what would have happened had he gotten farther. Tim rolled off of me. I sat up and untied the half-hitch from around my waist and gave a tug on the rope. It was free and easy to haul down until it fell down on top of us. We laughed our relief, and sat in the snow resting for several minutes. With the rope now free and in our hands, we had a chance again.

I carefully coiled the line and tied it off with a clove hitch to secure it, leaving enough line so that we could tie ourselves to each other. We rose to our feet.

11

Seen

Our climb that day was in a very sparsely populated portion of rural Alberta, Canada. In 1980, there were two million people living in all of Alberta, an area of roughly 255,000 square miles, and most of the population lived in the cities far to the south. Only one car drove down the parkway that night. We felt—and were—very alone. Even if a car did drive by, why, we asked ourselves, would anybody happen to look up to our spot and see us on this long range of mountains paralleling the parkway?

And yet, just before we tied ourselves off to each other for our next traverse to our rappel, we heard a vehicle heading south on the Icefields Parkway far below us. We stopped, watched, and waited, ever hopeful that we might be spotted. As the headlights came into view, we watched as the car slowed down and turned right into the parking lot where we'd left Tim's car. We guessed it was around midnight. We thought maybe the driver of the vehicle had seen Tim's car sitting there alone and was going to check it out. The vehicle slowly swung around and faced the mountainside, toward us, and with its head-lights still on, stopped.

We stomped to the edge of the cliff and jumped up and down, shouting and waving our arms high over our heads in the moonlight, hoping we would be seen. After an exhilarating but exhausting bit of movement, the driver flashed his headlights twice. We stopped jumping. He flashed his headlights again. We jumped again. He flashed again. He could see us!

We deduced that the driver must be the park ranger at whose cabin we'd spent a night. He must have realized that we had not signed out of his wilderness entry and exit registration log and had come to find us. We were heartened and felt a surge of joy. We laughed and dared to hope, though we were still in serious trouble stuck up on the ice climb. He could not save us, but he knew we were there.

Our exhaustion, exacerbated by our outburst of energy upon seeing the ranger's truck and our ever-advancing hypothermia made it difficult to walk. We tied ourselves to each other again for safety. Again, I had to take my gloves off to tie the knot. The cold bit deeply into my fingers. The ranger must have watched our sil-houettes as we traversed through the deep snow to the narrow icy and rocky trail that led beside the steep moun-tain face, walking with slow and deliberate steps toward our next rappel.

Tim turned to me and raised a finger to his lips, indicating that he was not going to speak unless nec-essary. As we felt our energy draining even further, we understood the desperate need to conserve our strength. Expending even a little might cause us to lose our lives. Survival was the only consideration. When he raised his finger to his lips, I told Tim, "Can't talk. Too tired. Too cold." Even without his voicing a reply, I knew that the same was true for him.

All night long we trusted each other in a way that I have never trusted anyone before or since. My life was in his hands, and his was in mine. During the hours of our tribulation, we each had withdrawn inside of ourselves out of necessity. My mind became 100 percent focused on one thing: driving my body to survival. Nothing else mattered.

We forced ourselves onward, forward. Each step took us closer to salvation at our last rappel, and then to the warmth of our tent. Yet, each step, because of the cold and our extreme exhaustion, also took us closer to death. We were balancing exhaustion and energy, fighting against our rapidly increasing hypothermia, and we both knew it. Once in a while, I looked down toward the ranger's truck. He sat there with his headlights on the whole time. He gave me hope, but I was still deeply, deeply afraid.

At one point during our traverse, I began to hear and feel my crampons scrape and clink on hard rock. The path itself was dark beneath our feet. I mostly walked by feel, with one mittened hand touching the mountain when I could. We entered the top of what appeared to be a boulder chute. The chute was our next rappel location. The top of the chute was bathed in moonlight, but most of it was in the dark shadow cast by the mountain, where the moonbeams could not reach. We took off our mittens without talking and untied ourselves.

Tim looped our rope through the iron O-ring that attached to an iron pin permanently hammered into the mountain face. We tested the strength of the O-ring and the pin for safety by pulling on the rope. As always, Tim led the way. He said, "I'll tug twice when I get to the bottom." I nodded and said nothing, watching as he disappeared among the boulders into the darkness. Once again alone, I leaned back against the mountain. I did not sit down for fear that I wouldn't have the energy to stand again. I was so cold, colder than I'd ever imagined I could be. There was no warmth in me at all. My feet hurt with cold; my hands hurt, my legs, and arms, and face, all hurt. I could feel the cold inside my brain. I kept a hand on our rope. After a time, I felt the two tugs. I tugged back twice. Tim replied with two more tugs. It was my turn.

I took my mittens off, felt the bite of the cold again, and concentrated on moving my fingers as my mind commanded them, willed them, to move, then watched them to make sure they did. I made my figure eight with my two locking carabiners and clipped our rope in. My path down on rappel was through the midst of huge boulders and crags, or at least that's what it felt like. I could not see much at all in the dark shadow cast by the mountain. I worked my way down slowly, trusting my rope, feeling with my feet, still colder than I thought humanly possible to survive, my mind still focused on a single drive: survive. I had no other thoughts.

In fact, my thought to survive did not feel like a thought at all. It was deeper than that. It was primal. All night long I kept digging deeper and deeper into my willpower, into my inner drive to live, into my inner resources, striving with a single-mindedness I had not known I possessed. I was devoid of energy. My thin body had already consumed what little fat I had, or so it felt. I felt empty, but I could keep going sheerly because of my mind and an inner strength greater than I'd known I had. I was surprised that it was there, but I imagine everyone has this and can find it when it is needed.

At the bottom of our rappel, I rounded the sharp-edged corner of the vertical cliff on my left and stepped to the narrow ledge where Tim waited for me. The ledge was narrower than the length of my boots and crampons. My heels hung over the edge. My toes touched the mountain face. My nose touched the rock.

I clipped my harness carabiner to the iron O-ring that was permanently iron-pinned into the mountain. Tim, to my left, had done the same. I looked at him. He smiled. We were safe for the moment and back in the moonlight. We turned to the ranger and waved. He flashed his headlights and, surprisingly, slowly drove out of the parking lot, turning left onto the parkway and then heading north.

We were alone again. My heart sank. We thought about this and spoke about it briefly, figuring that the ranger must have believed that we were safe enough with one single and easy rappel left, and close enough to the bottom to get there on our own; plus, he must have been tired and needed sleep. No doubt he was angry with us, too.

☞ 12 ☜

A Beautiful Place to Die

It was now an hour or two before dawn. Our tent, which was still packed inside Tim's car, was now 150 feet below us, ready to be set up, ready to give us shelter. We were exhausted beyond what I could have ever imagined for any human being; our energy was completely depleted. We were ravenously hungry, bitterly cold, frostbitten, blue-lipped, shivering to our marrow, yet driven to survive. I took my mittens off my frozen hands one more time, felt again the bite of the icy air in my fingers down to my bones, and tied one end of our climbing rope to my harness and dropped the bitter end into the darkness to my right, into the shadow of the chute. I pulled on my end.

Immediately, the rope jammed. I gave it a whip, hoping that would free the line. I pulled again. The rope jammed tighter and would not budge. With difficulty, my lips were barely able to move, I told Tim the rope was jammed.

It was a tricky situation. The bowline knot I had tied to connect the rope to my harness meant that the rope was too short for Tim to reach and help me pull. If

I untied the rope from my harness, Tim would be able to reach it and help me pull, but in our clumsy and frozen condition we might drop the rope. I had enough brain-power left to figure that out and told Tim, "If we drop the rope, we die." That was the bottom line. No rope, no survival. No rope, sure death.

We discussed this some, and with each word I could feel my remaining strength leave. It was almost as if I could measure my last drops of energy and see them leave my mouth. I had never before thought about how much energy it takes to think, to form words and sentences in the mind, and then speak them aloud. When one has nothing left for strength, that effort becomes clear.

We decided that we needed the rope to stay tied to me, and talked about an alternative: Tim could unclip his carabiner from his O-ring and inch along the rock face with his nose to the wall, then try clipping his carabiner into the same O-ring I was using. It was a brave and fool-ish idea. With his steel-cramponed heels hanging over the granite ledge, it was too dangerous of a maneuver for him to try to help free our rope. Without the protection of his carabiner clipped into the O-ring that was pinned into the mountain, and with no rope to save him, Tim would very likely fall to his death.

It was up to me. Getting the rope free was my job. In my weakened and failing condition, I pulled on our rope again, by myself. All night we had striven together as one force, as a team. Together, we would survive—that is what I chanted in my mind: *Together, we will survive*. It became my prayer.

And, now, that had changed. Our lives were in my leather-mittened hands. I continued to pull on the rope as hard as I could with all my remaining strength. The rope was completely jammed around the corner and lodged up in the dark. It did not budge, and my pulling may have jammed it tighter. I told Tim this. "Keep trying," he said. I kept pulling.

I thought about trying to trust the jam, thinking to swing out around the corner and try to reascend. It was a crazy thought, and when I told Tim, he told me so. The rope could un-jam under my weight, or as soon as I got around the corner; if it did, I would fall and die, and Tim, rope-less, would die too.

I had been so cold, so cold for so many hours. Then, rather suddenly, warmth swept though my entire body. For the first time since the morning before, I was actually hot. I was sweating. It was illogical. Rationally, I knew that my body was cold, but my torso and head were hot. I felt the blood drain from my arms and stop flowing toward my legs. I figured that my body knew that my limbs were expendable. I could lose my arms and legs, but my brain and heart and lungs—my core—must be saved if I was going to live.

This was a bad sign. "I'm hot," I told Tim. I unzipped my 60/40 jacket. It was crazy to open my jacket to try to cool down. I realized it was crazy, and despite feeling hot I zipped back up, or maybe Tim told me to zip up. I pulled on the rope again and again, but it still wouldn't budge. I kept whipping the rope up and down, up and down, then I pulled again. It was definitely stuck.

My mind and willpower remained hyperfocused on survival, but I stopped pulling and rested. I looked back over my left shoulder, away from the dark wall, up into the stunning beauty of the sky, and around at the gorgeous moonlit scenery in which we were immersed. At first I was afraid that I would not be able to save us, and then a surge of peace overtook me. I was no longer afraid. I was accepting my fate . . . my fate was death, and that was okay with me. I had tried. I had striven. We had striven, and we had failed.

My eyes took in what I thought would be my last view, my final sight: I could see the Columbia Icefield glistening in the moonlight. It was beautiful. I was warm. My mind was at ease. I knew the signs. A resignation and a self-admittance told me I was going to die there. I thought about my family, and how brokenhearted they would be when they found out I'd died. After my mom's breakdown, and the subsequent family suffering after my sister vanished from our lives, I wondered if in their coming grief they would be angry with me; and if their grief would crush them.

I said to myself, *This is a beautiful place to die.* And it was. I knew my death would be peaceful rather than violent. Freezing to death is peaceful, or so I had read. It is as peaceful as falling asleep, which I knew was about to come next. The rope was stuck. I was stuck. We were stuck, and there on that cliff the next morning, the first climber to arrive after first light would see our bodies. I was sorry about that and knew that we would be ruining someone's day.

Under that wide sky with its myriad brilliant, distant, and distinct stars shining and twinkling in a dozen colors, visible even under the bright moon that had risen ever higher throughout the night, I felt a complete and compelling peace about dying.

This surprised me. Feeling peaceful in the face of death felt like giving up. And I refused to give up. My willpower, my primal self, said, *NO! I will not quit. I will NOT die. Not here. Not tonight.*

The scene around us was beyond beautiful, indescribable, and I prayed again, but this time a different prayer. I said to God, and again to myself: *This is a beautiful place to die. I'm not quitting; but if I have to die tonight, I am content that it is in a most beautiful place.*

I pulled the rope again and again, and as I pulled sleep came for me. I began to feel so sleepy, so impossibly sleepy. I tried to stay awake. I tried to force myself to stay alert. I told myself, *This is not sleep. This is dying.* I dug deeper into myself to force myself to awaken, will myself to remain awake, but I was spent. I had no strength left.

As I began to fall asleep for the first time, I felt my knees buckle beneath me, and I could not stop them. I felt darkness close in around me, narrowing my vision. My eyes closed, and I could not force them back open. I felt my feet lose their footing, and felt myself fall. I swung down on my harness and carabiner and slammed, frozen face and helmeted head first, into the granite mountainside.

The hard blow against the mountain woke me. My face hurt. My head hurt. I climbed back up. Tim was speaking. I could hear him, but I couldn't understand what he was saying . . . nor did I care. I yanked on the rope. My world narrowed. My mind got smaller. I could not see or hear Tim at all, and I did not care that I could not. It didn't matter. All there was, was me, just me and the cold, the mountain, and the rope. Again I felt darkness encircle me, close in on me. I was aware of my sight narrowing, of darkness closing in like a fade to black in an old black-and-white film. Sleep overtook me, and I tumbled off my ledge.

I hit the rock face again, awoke again, and climbed up, and pulled the rope. I do not know how many times this happened—twice, thrice, or more—nor do I have any idea what Tim was doing at that time. It was all darkness to me. I lost track of time, and lost track of myself and the world around me. Darkness had closed in on me again. It was a struggle to see anything. The light of the night faded in my mind. The light of my mind faded to black. My vision narrowed. I felt my breathing slow down. Sleep was more powerful than my willpower to stay awake, than my willpower to survive. Each time I felt myself falling asleep, I dove even deeper into myself, willing myself to stay awake, but instead I slept. I fought sleep. I knew sleep was my end; yet, I could not stop it.

My years of first-aid training had helped me understand and explain to Tim the measure of trouble we were in at each stage of increasing hypothermia, and how much time we might have left as each stage encroached upon our bodies. It was macabre but necessary to keep track of our dying. Throughout the night, symptom by symptom, step by step, we watched as we strove to live, yet continued to succumb to exposure. Sleep is the end stage of dying from exposure. Hypothermia means too little heat. Sleep is death, and death is sleep. I knew that, did not want that. Every cell of my body screamed NO!, but I could not fight my body's demand for sleep. If I'm going to die, I told myself again, this is a beautiful place to do so.

☞ 13 ☜

Irresistible Pull

I felt myself slipping completely into darkness. I watched it envelop me like a sphere closing in. I could not stop it. My sight narrowed to a smaller and smaller circle of light until even that was crushed and closed by the overwhelming darkness. My body had failed me. My brain had failed. I had failed. I felt my last breath leave my body. I tried to take in one more and I could not. I had fought the closing darkness with all I had left inside me, but I was finally dying. I could feel it. I knew it. Inescapable death . . .

I could feel death. Such a strange thing it was to feel death, to feel my body fail and the world cease to be for me. The night and cold had killed me, and I was powerless to stop it. I was not the all-powerful and immortal youth I had believed I was. I was a human and I was dying, and that was life. Life will kill you.

I sensed my body fall off the ledge again, but this time I did not feel my face or head or body hit the wall. I had fallen asleep; I knew that. I was in the darkness and had fallen off my ledge; I knew that. I was confused because

I was awake in what *felt* like sleep. My mind should have faded to black, like every time it had ever since childhood whenever I fell asleep. I was in total darkness, but knew not where I was . . . except for the fact that I was not asleep. I was somehow awake inside an inner darkness. I was conscious; I was confused. *I should be asleep,* I thought. I knew that the mountain must be in front of me. It had to be, but I could not feel it, and I could not open my eyes to see it. Yet, with my eyes closed, I could suddenly see . . . but what I was seeing and what I was feeling were things I could not understand.

I saw and felt the darkness as if it was one thing: a greater darkness, a moving darkness, a living darkness. And it was moving toward me, moving at me. It came right at me, rapidly. It wanted me. It was coming for me. The feeling was like a soul-sucking vacuum, one with an overwhelming force of the most powerful gravity. Immediately, it was sucking *me* out of my body. I put up a shield of my will. I refocused all of my might to stop this thing from taking me. I did not know what it was. I only knew it wanted me. And I fought. I clung. I willed myself to stay.

But it was only a moment of will, only a moment of fight against such a tremendous power and unspeakable force. I was outmatched by a factor of ten trillion to one. My intense willpower and the inner strength I had honed through the night had gotten me to a single-minded state of bestial survival, but it seized me anyway, broke through my fragile defenses. It happened fast. It took me and I released, because I had no choice. I was like a leaf caught up in a great flood. It took me, and I felt it meant to take me. I sensed it had the intention to take, and in some strange way, deep, deep down inside myself, I knew that it must. It was not a thing. It was no thing. It had no form. It was not of this world. It had no molecules, no chemicals, no DNA, no cells, no particulars or any other thing that I could begin to describe or read about or conceive. It was no thing. Not a thing. It was other. I had to go. I could not stay.

The Power plucked me. It plucked the real me, the whole me, the holy whole soul me. Until that moment I had never fully understood the soul of me—the who/what/why that are the real whole of me. I had thought that I was body and soul. Suddenly, I knew that this was not the case. I was only soul. My body was simply where I had dwelled. I suddenly, fully, completely knew that what I was, what I am, who I am, and what I will be forever and eternally is soul. Soul was me. Soul is me. My body was not me. It never had been me. My body housed my soul, and when I was plucked from my flesh, I was still *me*.

This is the hardest part of my story to write because nothing I will say from here on out can be verified, quantified, or qualified. Why? Because on the other side I had no body, no brain, no blood, no bones, no eyes, no fingers, no toes, no culture, no language, no anything that is a thing in this world.

Without a brain, there is no language. Without language, how can one say what one saw or heard or felt? I could see, but had no eyes—or maybe I had ten thousand eyes, because I could see in every direction all at once. I could hear when spoken to, but I had no ears; furthermore, there was no voice or sound—yet, I could hear.

On the other side, there is no thing. Everything on this side, in the world in which we live, is a thing. Over there, nothing is a thing. There is no thing. Language cannot describe it. Language cannot contain it.

I am compelled to talk about it now; yet, paradoxically, I know no words can convey it. This no-thing is so present to me now as I write that it overwhelms me. I cannot escape it. This overwhelming feeling has filled my days, every day, ever since that night. In the years since my death I have done my best to say what cannot be said, to articulate what cannot be articulated, to describe what cannot be described, and think about what cannot be thought about.

Three years after my experience, I went to Yale Divinity School in order to find some language that might help me frame what happened to me. And so, here it is: God is no thing. I repeat: God is no thing. God is not a thing. Anything that can be said about God is inaccurate. Words are things. God is not. God cannot be explained, contained, described, or even seen.

☙ 14 ☙

The Voice

I found myself in a vast, infinite darkness, in a place that was not a place, a place that was outside of time, and eternal, a place where there is no thing—and, yet, I was a being . . . spherical, sort of, and I had life, but no breath. I was me, and I knew I was me, yet I had no flesh and no bones. It was curious, and I was unafraid. I could think, and, as best I could, comprehend that I was still me. Better yet, I had no brain to interfere with my thinking. I was *life*, or energy, or soul. I was a being. My body was a ball of soul, a being ball, a ball of being. I was I. I could see, but I had no eyes. It was as if I could see with ten thousand eyes, or one eye in every direction at once. I was floating, and yet firmly in a Vast Darkness—a Greater Darkness that extended beyond sight in every direction. But the Darkness was not dark. I could see it. I floated and was stable in the Darkness, and I was alone.

A gigantic doorway or gateway appeared, or maybe it was there all along and I'd just not seen it yet. This is what the entire experience was like: Maybe it had all been there my entire life, just beyond my vision, and I simply could not see it. (Note: I'm using words to describe what I remember, but remember I had no brain, nor had I language; neither exists on the other side.) It was timeless there—I tell my story in this order because words must be placed sequentially, but there was no sequence of events. All I experienced may have happened at once.

The gateway, the doorway was a hundred yards high and seventy yards across if I had to guess. I could see a long, arching tunnel of darkness; it was very, very dark leading from the gateway to God-knows-where. The gateway and its tunnel or corridor pierced the Greater Darkness and was contained within it but seemingly led beyond it, or through it somehow. The doorway itself was shimmering and flowing, like a waterfall, only it was not water, and was simultaneously translucent and transparent. I reached out with my being to touch the shimmer, to feel it . . . and I did. I touched the shimmer with something like a hand, but I had no hand. The shimmer was Alive. The gateway was Alive. I felt the Life in it. It was Living Energy. I felt the energy of Life flowing in the shimmer and I felt it flow into me.

Simultaneously, I heard my name called from deep, deep inside of me, and yet also from beyond me. I heard my name called, and it was not just my name Peter, or Pete, or Petie, or Petro, or any of the names I was called by those who knew me and loved me. It was Peter and more: It was my soul's name, and it was said with Love beyond imagination, beyond comprehension. It was Love that was Real, and Love that is Reality. It was my true name, my real name, and the name that revealed *me* to me. It was and is my name that only God can speak. I heard my name come from outside of myself but heard it inside myself, but it was not a word. At least, it was not spoken as a word in any way that I can say. Yet, it was me: I was in the word, and the word, my name, was who I was.

The scriptures teach us that to know the true name of a person is to have power over them. This is what happens in the story where Jacob wrestles with the angel and demands to know the angel's name. On the other side, my true name was called to me. I was called by my true name, and thus was completely and utterly in the power of the Being that called my name. I belonged to the One who made me, and suddenly I knew the truth of that and what it meant.

My name was, and I suppose still is, the essence of my being, the ground of my *self*, the light of me, and the whole of life. There were no words spoken. There was no language. There was no sound. The Voice that called my name came from outside me, and was present to me and nearby, yet distant as well. I could not see the Voice, but instead felt Its immanence and immensity. It was not my voice that I heard, nor the voice of my unconscious or my conscience. I heard the Voice of the Almighty deep inside my soul, beneath me, around me, beyond me, and the Voice filled me with my name—and, in the filling, knew me in totality.

The Voice knew me fully and completely and there was no part of me that was unknown. I was revealed, fully revealed, in all my beauty and hideousness. Nothing could be hidden; nothing of me was hidden. I had no choice in the matter. I was fully and completely known, and that was that. All of me, the whole of me, everything about me was completely contained inside my name. In saying the name, I was known. And, in hearing my name, I knew that I was known. It was my true name that only God knows, and only God can say. Every action, every love, every hate, every sorrow, every joy, every tear, and every smile was there, and there were no dark and hidden corners with me. When I heard my name, I was revealed, and I knew God was completely present.

How did I know it was God? I just knew that it was, and it could be no other. I knew because God told me so in the very calling of my name. I knew that the Knower knew me. It was instantaneously obvious that my Creator was there with me, calling my true name that I heard inside myself, inside my soul. I was creature; I knew in that moment I was made by my Maker. I was a created being made by the Uncreated.

I understood that God was right there beside me, and fully with me, although I could not see God at all. God had no being but was all Being. I could still see the Greater Darkness, and the gateway, but my sight turned within. I was on the doorstep, the threshold of heaven, and I knew to the core of my soul that it was YHWH who spoke. The Voice that spoke without sound or language communicated with me telepathically. The Voice was neither male nor female, neither old nor young. The Voice was pure and holy, and only Love, Only Love and Beauty, and Light, Almighty, Maker. There was total and complete communication without words, unencumbered by language. I heard with my soul-mind; I heard with the ear of my soul; I heard with all of my being, I heard with my soul. Seeing, hearing, being, feeling, thinking was all one to me.

My true name filled me; it in-filled me. The Voice in-filled me like a breath with a gift undeserved of Love-Hope-Joy-Beauty-Truth-Charity-Kindness-Compassion-Love-Patience-Beauty-Love, and it was all one indescribable, amalgamated combination. The gift was heaven filling up inside my soul-being, inside of me, the true and real me. I was on what I think of as the threshold of heaven, at the gateway, the proverbial pearly gate, and God gave me the undeserved gift of heaven within me. In this world of ours, here on earth, we separate Love-Hope-Joy-Beauty-Truth-Charity-Kindness-Compassion-Love-Patience-Beauty-Love into differentiated things. We individualize them. We have truth. We have love. We have beauty. We have joy. We have hope. We have charity. Each is a separate idea or action or experience, and sometimes they overlap. Not so in heaven. In heaven they are One; they are One-ness, and they emanate from the Divine who is Oneness.

I was in-filled, overfilled, completely filled, spilling over with this Oneness, this Love-Hope-Joy-Beauty-Truth-Charity-Kindness-Compassion-Love-Patience-Beauty-Love—this Unity. I became the Love-Hope-Joy-Beauty-Truth-Charity-Kindness-Compassion-Love-Patience-Beauty-Love. It was and is indescribable, and yet even with this heaven within me, I was still just me, soul-Peter—I knew who I was, and I knew that I was *known*, fully, completely, and utterly *known*, completely naked to my Maker who could see every part of me. I was naked. That is the word. Naked. Exposed. Seen. And I was loved beyond imagination, beyond comprehension.

☞ 15 ☞

My Hell

The divine in-filling flooded me with knowledge. I suddenly knew and understood so many things I had not comprehended on earth. Eventually, when I returned to my flesh body, to my earth body, I remembered only that I had once known so very much more, but that I now no longer understood or comprehended what had been shown to me in heaven. I now know only that I did once know, no longer knew, and expectedly will know once more when I die again.

And then came hell. (Again, dear reader, I tell this story as if it happened in a sequence, but time did not exist. There was no sequence there, only eternity. This is the sequence that I first told my story on that Sunday morning, and because of that I think maybe it occurred this way, though perhaps it did happen at once, which is more likely.)

Hell. I entered my own hell. It was hell inside me, my personal hell. It was, it turns out, the hell I had created for myself; or, rather, my own hell entered into me, overtook me, owned me, and filled me. It was my personal hell because I saw that I had created it second by second, minute by minute, hour by hour, day by day, month by month, and year by year while I lived enfleshed. I made my own hell, and it was horrifying.

I had not known that I had been busy creating my own hell while I was alive. I did not know I carried my own hell within me as my loathsome treasure. As I reflect on this part of my death, I see in my mind's eye the ghost of Jacob Marley from Charles Dickens's *A Christmas Carol*. Marley wore the chains he had forged in life link by link. I had forged my own hell, action by action. My birth—during which I caused my mother much pain—was not included in my self-judgment; neither was the period when I was an innocent newborn. Are we not all born the same—innocent?

Let me explain: The hell I suffered was to see, hear, feel, understand, and embody all of the pain I had ever caused during my earthly life to anyone I had known, from their point of view. I had carried their pain with me and brought their pain with me into the afterlife. How unexpected. It was a record, a file, a folder, a book of life somehow written and recorded inside my soul. God had not done this to me. God had not caused my hell. I saw that immediately. I had done it to myself. I had woven it on my own. I had burned each wrong action onto my own DVD, and yet it was also clear to me that my brokenness was simply a part of being a human being.

To cause pain to another was, or so it appeared to me, the natural order of life on earth. I was not special; I was not unique in that regard. I had just been a human and did what all human beings do to each other. We hurt each other. The hurting is sin.

I felt their pain, the pain I had unwittingly caused and the pain I had freely and often purposefully given to some persons, particularly the ones I loved—my mother, my father, my sisters, my brother, my friends, but my classmates, acquaintances, and strangers, too. They were all there—every one and every instance.

I witnessed and suffered every instance of pain, every instance of sin since the moment of my birth, in rapid and full sequence. I felt their pain, the pain that I had caused them to feel, and it was overwhelming, like a painful yet purifying fire in my soul. Every hurt I had ever caused, big or small, intended or unintended, was piled up for me to see and feel and experience. I had sinned. I had never really even understood what sin was; I had denied that sin really existed. But suddenly I knew what sin was: Sin was and is causing another to hurt. Sin was unavoidable. Sin was inevitable. Many of my sins were unintentional, accidental, actions I'd taken that I'd never known might cause hurt. I knew I had sinned, and now I understood the full meaning of this.

It is odd to me that of all the understanding I gained on the other side and have forgotten, this one thing I remember so well. Sin was the hurt that I had given or caused in my lifetime. In my own hell, I suffered all of the pain that I had cast on others, from the smallest pain to the largest, intentionally given or unintentional. Hell was not outside of me; it was not a place to go to—it was a place within. My hell drowned out the Love-Hope-Joy-Beauty-Truth-Charity-Kindness-Compassion-Love-Patience-Beauty-Love that had been in me—and left me filled with shame. Further, for each sin, each and every pain I had ever caused, I also simultaneously witnessed and felt all of my inadequate justifications, my weak reasoning, my causations for giving each individual every pain that I had given them. I was my own judge. I held the scale of my guilt, and my fate.

I saw my inadequacies—all of them. Every single circumstance was accounted for, even those in which I had harbored no ill will, had no intention to cause hurt, or had not even known that I had caused pain. These two things—feeling all the pain I had ever caused in my life juxtaposed with witnessing all my paltry justifications—led me to self-judgment . . . and I judged myself guilty. I was guilty. I had sinned greatly.

I was utterly ashamed of myself. The evidence against me, created by me, was within me, and I was overwhelmed. I had no defense. There was no defense. In the face of Great Love I was nothing, and had nothing with which to defend myself. I was guilty as charged. My reasons, my justifications, my causations for causing hurt weighed nothing on my scale when compared with the immense pain I had caused in my twenty-one years of life. I was guilty. I knew it. I believed it. My hell was repulsive and abhorrent. Hell hurt. Hell held no beauty, and no love, only truth. My hell was the most pain I had ever suffered. It was the pain of others.

And yet, there was a third simultaneous perspective even as I experienced my own hell. It was the Voice of God, the Love of God spoken to soothe my passage through hell, speaking to me and within me from outside of me but without language. It was the Voice of God that I heard, repeatedly assuring me, *I love you, Peter. I know you, Peter. I made you, Peter. You are my creature, Peter. I know all about you, Peter. Nothing is hidden from me. I have always known all about you. I know you did all of this. I see all. I see all of you. I love you. I made you. You are my creature. I love you. I forgive you. I forgive you. I forgive you.*

And suddenly, undeservedly, I was forgiven fully and completely and instantaneously. I deserved no mercy. I had judged myself guilty, and I was guilty; I was worthy of punishment. That was truth. I was soulfully ashamed of myself—perhaps that is what saved me, my shame, or perhaps not. Perhaps God, the Unseen, the Merciful, the Almighty, forgave me completely and burned away all of my sin in my own hell simply because I am beloved, just as you are beloved, just as each and every one of us is beloved. All I know is that I was made whole and holy again. All the pain I had caused vanished. My hell ended; my need for hell ended. I passed through, and because of Love, I was once more in-filled with Love-Hope-Joy-Beauty-Truth-Charity-Kindness-Compassion-Love-Patience-Beauty-Love. I was loved, and knew I was loved by the Lover.

‿ 16 ‿

God Is Love

Heaven and hell all happened inside my mind/soul/ being. There were neither words nor even a voice, per se. It was all communicated directly to me telepathically. I knew I had no brain to process the information; yet, strangely, I could think more clearly and understand more clearly than I ever had or have since. My brain was not getting in the way of my thinking, as it is now. I am dyslexic with ADD; I am an American; I speak English— and none of these attributes, or anything else, interfered with my thinking on the other side. I was simply beloved creature, fully known and fully loved, and I was gratefulness itself, and worshipful completely.

From inside my soul-self, I spoke to God without words or language, through pure thought, and asked, *Am I dead?*

God said, *Yes. You are dead.*

I heard this inside my soul, inside myself, but I knew that it had been spoken to me, or more accurately *thought* to me, from outside myself, from God who was present but whom I could not see. How did I know it was God?

I just knew. It was self-evident. Another thing that was self-evident was that I had carried into the afterlife all the love I had given away and all the love I had ever gathered. All of that love—given and gathered—was my treasure. While there were two types of love that I had with me (given and gathered), they seemed also to be simultaneously one love.

I thought to God, *I haven't gone through the door yet, and I can't go through the door* (referring to the gateway that I somehow knew led to a deeper heaven).

God asked, *Why not?*

I should have wondered why God, who knew me thoroughly, did not know the answer to this. It seemed natural that God should ask this question of me and that I should have a chance to answer in my own way.

I answered, *My sister Andrea ran away when I was young. Andrea just vanished. She broke my mother's heart. My mother still has a broken heart. It ruined my mother's life and affected her health. My father also has a broken heart and a lot of anger because of what Andrea's running away did to her mother, to her siblings, and to him. We kept her absence a secret from everybody except family. I cannot be the one who takes another child away from them. I cannot break their hearts that way again. It would crush them, and wound them so that they might never recover. They have not recovered from Andrea. It would devastate them. I love them too much for that. I cannot go. I cannot.*

Suddenly, God took me, carried me or swept me, to a high place and showed me all of earth all at once from a great distance, and yet I could see all the people on earth individually and all at once, all together. In particular, my focus landed on my mother and father, whom I could see up close and clearly. I could see their broken, loving hearts inside of them. I could see all of their suffering and sorrow, their pain, their wounds, anger.

God said to me, *I love you.*

I said, *I know.*

God said, *I love you more deeply than your imagination could ever have conceived. I know you and love you, Peter. You are my creature. Because you are here, now you know how much I love you, and you know how great my love is.*

I said, *Yes, God, I know You love me, personally and infinitely more than I could have ever conceived or imagined. I feel like your beloved, your special one, and more than that. I feel Your love as the greatest love beyond what I can even contain or hold within me.*

God's love was so wide and deep, so full and sweet, so safe and eternal. It was so much greater than any love I had ever felt before, and yet somehow I knew I had always been loved in this way by God for my entire life, even when I was in my physical body and could not feel the fullness of that great love. I knew I was always beloved.

God said to me, inside me, without language, *In the way I love you now I have always loved you, and will always love you. You know.*

I knew that was the Truth. I knew I was beloved as a particular person, individually, and specially, as if I was the only one who mattered. That is how it felt, and yet it also felt that God's great love for me was not exclusive to me, that God loved every human being in exactly the same way. It felt that God is, was, and always will be love.

God continued, *In the way I love you now, and you know that I love you, I also love everyone, every human being, every person on earth, right now, always—and I love your mother and your father in this same way. Because I love your parents in the same way that I love you, in the way that you now understand I have always loved you, forever and eternally, all has been well, all is well, and all will be well with them, and for everyone, because of My love.*

I could see, sense, feel, taste, hear, and know to the core of my soul the very Truth of God's eternal love for me, for my parents, and for all of humanity. God's love was, is, and will be forever real, eternal, and lasting. I knew that for my parents, at their death, all would be well. I knew this because at my own death all was well, and love made me whole and holy, worthy, and acceptable.

None of this was my doing. All of it was God's doing, from God's love. All of my suffering had ended, and I understood that eventually, when my parents died, when they stepped outside of time, that their suffering would end too, permanently; that their sorrow, sense of loss, and anger would vanish, and joy and love and healing and wholeness and holiness would be in them, just like it was in me. My loving God had healed me, fully, totally, and completely to the core of my being. I was imbued with love and joy. My parents would also be healed upon their deaths. However, I also knew and understood that until they died their suffering in life would continue—and were I to stay on in heaven, I understood that their suffering would be ever more painful.

Life's a Wink and Heaven Is Beauty

Although God had no eyes that I could see, I could sense God wink at me—and in the wink show me that my entire life, the lives of my parents, and the lives and times of all humans on earth encompass just the wink of God's eye. My life and your life are as brief as the quick wink of God's eye. The illusion is that we have all the time in the world, but time itself is an illusion. We have little time. Life on this planet is brief. In that amount of time, just a wink, my life began, was lived, and ended. The same is true for you, although it does not feel that way.

I understood that time and life on the planet, in the world we call earth and galaxy and universe were not real in the way that God is Real. Only God is Real; all else is both real and an illusion. All of my life, from my birth to death, all twenty-one years of it, was a mere blink when compared with eternity. God showed me that as a creature, as one created by my Creator, as one who is made and not self-made, that all lifetimes—mine, yours, our mother's and father's, everybody's—are so fast. They start, and they are over. I know it does not seem like that on this side, in this world. Only in death, when eternity opens, when timelessness is normative, does it become clear just how brief life is. Time is an illusion. Eternity is Real. God is Real.

Even knowing that I was beloved eternally, and knowing that my parents were beloved, and that they would be healed of suffering at their death as I was healed—even knowing all of that, I said, *I still cannot stay here.*

As if Omnipotent did not know the reason, God asked me, *Why?*

I replied, *God, I'm in a college theater troupe. We leave on a 24,000-mile, 64-show tour in one week. The director of the Theater of Silence, and my communications professor in American Sign Language at Montana State University, had actually grabbed me by the shirt collar when he heard I was headed into the Canada wilderness to go backcountry camping and ice climbing for spring break and, with his face in my face, said to me, 'Peter, do not get hurt next week. There are no understudies. You can't be replaced. The show must go on. Be careful.' I promised him that I would be careful and that I would be ready for the tour.* I told all of that to God in a single thought.

With compassion and love God said, *You do not have to come Home now if you do not want to.*

I asked, *Is this heaven?* I was referring to heaven living inside my soul (and me contained within it)—the wholeness, the holiness, the being known by God with absolutely no secrets, and the safety and security of that overwhelming Love-Hope-Joy-Beauty-Truth-Charity-Kindness-Compassion-Love-Patience-Beauty-Love that was, in God's presence, my complete self. I was whole and holy in the presence of God, and as beautiful as it was, and as true as God's words were, I felt as if I had a responsibility on earth, to my parents and to my theater troupe. I was not done with life. I had commitments. I had work to complete, and family not to hurt.

God said, *Yes, this is heaven that you feel, that you are because of Me, living within you. You do not have to die now; you do not have to stay here. You can go back if you want to go back.*

I knew that to be the Truth. I said, *If I go back to earth, to my body, to my life, to my family, then the next time I die, may I come back here to this Beauty-Love, to this heaven of healing and wholeness, this mercy and forgiveness, this Compassion-Joy and Truth? If I choose to live my life, will I come back here? Will I come back to you?*

God was heaven, and heaven was God, and God was greater than heaven. The two were one, yet separate. God gave me heaven. It was beauty and love beyond compare. I did not deserve it, but I was so grateful to be there. And yet, I was bold enough to ask to leave.

God said, *Yes, Peter, my beloved, you can come back to Me.*

I said, *I choose to live my life.*

God said, *Peter, my beloved, you won't live your life.*

And with those words, God sent me away.

⌐ 18 ⌐

Alien in My Body

The next thing I knew and felt was searing pain. It felt like I was being slowly and painfully twisted, like an ice screw, back into my physical body at that point above my stomach and below my heart. I was stuffed back into my body, and it hurt. I hurt all over. I awoke. I was me, but I did not know what I was, who I was, where I was, or what I was doing. My body was dangling on my harness at an angle, and I could hear a voice shouting. I was dazed and disoriented. I did not understand anything. I was back in the world inside a body that I did not understand. I opened my eyes and looked up at the man who was screaming at me and looking right at me. I wondered, *Who is he? Where am I? Why is he yelling?*

Then, he had a hand on me, was grasping my jacket hood and pulling on me, jerking me, trying to hoist me up, or wake me up, or something. I watched him dispassionately for a time, as if I was observing him from afar, while trying to figure out what I was: What was this thing—this body—that I was in? Who was I? Where was I? What is this being—this man thing—who is yelling words at me that I do not comprehend while yanking on me?

Minutes passed, and I slowly understood that I was back in my body. Then, I recognized Tim. Bit by bit, I understood: I was Peter. I was a human being and no longer just a soul. I was on a mountain. My body hurt. I had not been hurting before.

Tim was shouting at me. He was very loud. He screamed at me, "DON'T DIE! DON'T DIE. WAKE UP! WAKE UP! DON'T DIE AND LEAVE ME HERE! DO NOT DIE! WAKE UP! IF YOU DIE, I WILL DIE."

Tim was crying, and shouting, and there was fear in his voice; but there was determination, too. I looked at his eyes, into his eyes, and saw that he saw that I was awake, and so he pulled harder on my shoulder. I clambered back up onto the ledge, disoriented. I watched him in the moonlight. He was still shouting and crying, saying, "I thought you were dead. I thought you were dead. I'm so glad you're not dead. You scared me. I was alone."

I said nothing. I could say nothing. I was having a difficult time thinking. I still didn't understand what I was or what had just happened to me. I remembered where I had been, but I didn't understand anything about it. I was perplexed, and struggled to figure out how my body worked, and even what my body was. One thing I did know was that I was not my body. I knew I was something inhabiting a body and that although it was somehow "me," it was also not me at all.

I stopped listening to Tim and focused on inhabiting this thing, this body I was in. After a while, I figured out how to move. I figured out where I was and who I was and what I was doing there. It all felt so alien, as if I were in a film against my will. I was disassociated from my body and everything around me, but I was also definitely in my body. It felt, I felt, like a contradiction. I looked down and saw the rope hanging from my harness and picked it up with both hands. It was instinctive rather than thoughtful. I turned away to look at the rope and saw it disappear around the corner of the cliff, and I pulled it hard. My hands hurt. My feet hurt. My face, my ears, my cheeks, my nose, my entire body hurt. Though I could barely make sense of anything, I pulled the rope hard . . . and the rope pulled free.

Tim cheered. The rope that had been stuck for God knows how long—hours?—suddenly on that one pull came free, and so I hauled it down, easy as could be. Tim whooped in joy. I began to remember who I was, or at least who I was as a body, and my mind started to make sense of all that was around me. Tim was talking excitedly, saying, "I thought you were dead. I thought I was going to die, too." I didn't know what to say. That I had been dead? That I had been somewhere else and in that somewhere else I had been me, but the me that I truly am, the soul me, the without-flesh me? I did not understand how to articulate my experience. I only knew that I had died, and I was no longer dead. Tim did not believe in God. How could I possibly talk with him about what I'd experienced? I could not.

Everything was different, as if I had been born again. And, in that second time, I knew that I was not real, and that the world was some sort of temporary illusion in which I was stuck and through which I was passing. I felt like I was in an alien world inhabiting a body that was not me, and that Tim could not see who I really was. He could only see what he thought I was.

But the rope was free, and all of those thoughts had to wait. I was no longer desperate to get off the mountain. Dying was hard, but death was beautiful . . . and the world was not. I no longer feared death, not at all. I was dispassionate about the world; I wanted to go back. I had made a choice: I had chosen this world and life here, but I knew deep down that I had made a tremendous mistake. I did not belong here. I was not from here. I wanted only to go back to God. Tim was my responsibility, though. He still feared dying. I needed to stay with him and help him, but had I been alone I know I could have unclipped. I could have just unclipped right there.

I thought about it—unclipping, leaning back slightly, and falling. The fall would surely have killed me, or killed my body. I did not want to be in this world, but I had a responsibility to Tim, to my troupe, and to my parents.

We had been standing on that narrow ledge for hours, fighting to save our lives—that much I understood. I also knew I had been dead, and that I'd been in heaven, or at least on heaven's threshold . . . but where was that? What had happened to me? How long had I been dead? I did not know.

I tried to focus on the task at hand, but it was difficult. My mind kept flying back to where I had just been. It felt as if the greater part of me was still there. I felt bifurcated, divided, not wholly in the world. It felt, it still feels, as if I had one foot here, and the other there. I knew that, moments before, I had been without a body, yet here I was in a body. I had been in God's overwhelming presence, and the Voice had spoken to me. I understood that the smartest I had ever been was when I had no brain. I had a brain again, and that confused me. I was aware that I had known and understood infinitely more only moments before than I now knew as I stood under the moonlight. I also knew that all I had just known moments before had slipped away as I reentered my body.

It was all so confusing and disorienting. I was lost, and so alone. I craved one thing: God, in fullness, in joy, and love, and truth, and beauty. I knew that I'd had all of that, and I had let it all go. *What a fool I am! What a fool I am to have come back*, I thought.

I ran the rope's bitter end through the iron O-ring that was iron pinned into the rock of the mountain cliff, and then threw both bitter ends down. "I'll go first," I said to Tim, and I rappelled our final 150 feet. Upon reaching the bottom my feelings were mixed. I was exhausted and only wanted warmth, food, and sleep. I was glad to be down, but I did not want to be there. I landed on the top of the partially snow-covered talus cone. (A talus cone is the accumulation of rocks, gravel, and dirt caused by erosion and found at the base of very steep mountains.) I waited and watched as Tim rappelled down next. After he was standing beside me, he pulled the rope down, quickly coiled it, and slung it over his shoulder. Silently, we picked our way down the steep slope to the flat, snow-covered ground.

➤ 19 ➤

Warden's Worry

W e were still suffering from exposure, but glad to be off the mountain as we headed toward Tim's truck. His tent and our packs were still in it. I could hardly think, and barely walk. Our bodies were worn out and still dying. Tim found his keys with frozen fingers and unlocked the trunk. We resisted the temptation to rest in the car with the heater on high—heating up too quickly is a bad idea when recovering from hypothermia, and the shelter of our tent, some tea, and our sleeping bags seemed like the better choice. So we shouldered our backpacks and trudged back across the Icefields Parkway to set up camp away from the base of Lower Weeping Wall.

We unpacked the tent and, with little communication, efficiently set it up in the moonlight, found our flashlights, turned them on, and pushed our backpacks inside the tent. We climbed into the tent and unrolled our sleeping pads on the floor, unstuffed our down sleeping bags, clumsily stripped off our wet clothes, and climbed naked inside our bags. I remember thinking that our best chance would be to zip our bags together and climb in together. We did not do this, though we should have.

Holding my little yellow flashlight between my teeth, as was my habit, I unpacked and set up my backpacking stove, filled it with white gas from my gas tank, pumped up the stove's tank, and fired it up with my Bic lighter. Meanwhile, Tim zipped the tent shut, popped up the chimney vent on the tent's roof, and opened the floor vent for ventilation. That way, we could fire up the stove inside the tent without adding asphyxiation as a danger. It was a large winter tent with enough room for our backpacks and both of us. Tim unzipped the tent door and reached outside to fill our large aluminum cooking pot with snow to melt for water. I put the pot on the stove as the tent began to warm up from the roaring blue flame. We waited in silence and shivered.

I pulled out some dry long underwear and wool socks and put them on. Tim did the same. The water steamed. I dropped a couple of Tetley tea bags into the simmering pot. We did not want boiling water, only *warm* water so as to gently raise our body temperatures. We did not wait for it to steep. We filled our plastic camp cups over and over, sipping the warm tea. We melted more snow and drank a lot more tea. As we warmed up, we gnawed on hard backpacker's bread and ate spoonfuls of peanut butter squeezed from our plastic backpacker's tubes. We dipped the peanut butter in the raisins we'd bought in Jasper two days before. We huddled close together for warmth, then lay down and nodded off.

Sometime after sunup, we were warm enough and we awoke. The tent was warm. The stove was out. I refilled the tank and fired it up as Tim got more snow to melt. We drank more tea—hot tea this time—and ate instant oatmeal with a dollop of honey and some boiled raisins on top. We talked little. We were still exhausted. Every extremity of my body ached and burned.

After breakfast, we pulled on dry clothes and put on our extra mittens and cross-country ski boots, crawled out of the tent on our hands and knees, and greeted a sunny, cold, and clear morning. We were alone. I put on my dark glasses to ward against the bright sun and snow reflection, and stared up at Lower Weeping Wall. It was a quiet, windless morning. We traced our climbing route up, our traverse across, and our rappelling routes down with our eyes. My eyes lingered on the ledge where we first sat at the top of our climb, and then on the lone tree at the top of our first rappel. I looked at the overhang below that tree and the edge of the ledge where we were when the ranger saw us. The traverse to our next rappel was narrow and, given the angle, I could see little of the boulder-filled crag that was our second rappel. When my eyes got to the narrow ledge on which I died, I just looked and looked. Tim jostled my shoulder. Apparently, I had been looking for some time and he'd been speaking to me, but I had not heard him.

It was frightening to see what we had survived. I was still completely confused about what had happened. Had it happened? Was it real? Had I died? What had I experienced? Was I crazy? Had the cold driven me temporarily mad? I felt that I was living simultaneously in two places, as if I was seeing what was before me—the snow, the mountain, the ice, the trees, the climb, and Tim—with one eye, while my other eye seemed to see something beyond, and it focused there, in another world, in another dimension, in a place more real than reality. I suddenly felt bereft and homeless.

Those feelings are with me still, more than thirty years later. I knew, at the time, that I could not explain any of it to my dear atheist friend to whom I had just trusted my life and, before I died, my inner thoughts. Besides, it all seemed like madness to me. I felt that I had touched upon insanity, and surely if I spoke of it aloud to my dear friend, he would not understand. What's more, I myself did not understand—and how could I talk about what I did not understand? I felt more lost and confused than I'd ever felt in my life.

Tim shook my shoulder again. "Come on," he said.

The air was crisp, and my feet and hands were getting cold again. They hurt again. They would hurt again for the rest of my life—every day that the temperature dropped below fifty degrees. That pain functions as a constant reminder of that day.

I was warmer, but my core was still cold. We decided to get on the road as soon as we could. We pulled everything out of the tent, stuffed our sleeping bags, packed our gear, collapsed the tent, then packed that too. Tim and I shouldered our backpacks and our climbing gear for what we thought was the last time in this wilderness, and walked out on the snow-packed path to the side of the Icefields Parkway. We dropped our backpacks by the roadside. Tim walked over to the car while I waited. It started up right away. He drove it over and left it running so that it would be warm when we got in.

As we loaded our gear into the open trunk, we heard a pickup truck coming down the highway. It was the first vehicle we'd seen that morning. The truck pulled up right behind us and stopped. It was the ranger—our ranger. He got out. We waited for him to approach and said hello.

"Boys, were you the two guys on the mountain last night?"

"Yes, sir," we said.

"I watched you last night from my truck in the parking lot. You saw me?"

"Yes, sir, and thank you. You gave us hope."

"I came down here this morning to see if you were alive, or if we had to go get the helicopter to recover your bodies off the mountain. I'm glad you survived. You two take care now," he said, shaking his head.

We shook hands, said good-bye, and then the ranger turned back to his truck, got in, and drove back north. He left us quietly pondering the truth of what he had said. We might have survived. Or, he might have had to dispatch the helicopter and team to recover our bodies; we would have made the news as the two dead climbers from Montana, and our parents would have been brokenhearted. We were humbled by his question and shaken by his statements.

We climbed into Tim's car and drove south. We did not talk much. We were both too exhausted. I offered to drive again. Tim said no, that his dad would not let anybody drive the car except him, adding that I knew that already and shouldn't bother asking again. That much had not changed. But I was changed. I was a different person. I was not the same man I'd been just the day before.

I knew I was Peter Panagore. I had all of my memories and feelings about the people I loved, but I no longer knew who—or what—I was anymore. I was from another dimension, another place. Earth was no longer my home. The part of me that was still in heaven was the real part of me; the part of me on earth was the lost part. I did not want to be in this body; hence, I did not want to be alive. Everything around me, everything I could see was flat, black-and-white, cartoonish, two-dimensional, and—despite the great beauty of the Canadian Rockies that morning—everything looked ugly and crass.

☞ 20 ☜

Bad Ride and Jail

I rode shotgun and watched the world out the window in silent reflection until I fell asleep. Sometime after dark, I awoke still in the car. I looked out the window into blackness then looked over at Tim. There was a jazz cassette playing in the tape deck. We had been listening to jazz since we left Bozeman. Jazz was new to me, and I liked it. Jazz still speaks to me, and for me, thanks to Tim. I looked at the road ahead as we sped south. Tim must have been really exhausted, because he had slept as little the night before as I had and had not slept at all during the day. The road ahead was dark except for a pair of headlights coming toward us . . . coming directly at us.

"Tim," I said, "I think you are on the wrong side of the road. Those headlights are headed straight at us."

Tim said, "I'm not on the wrong side of the road. You just woke up. You don't know what you are seeing."

I scanned the road intensely, believing him. But I was sure of what I was seeing; he was wrong. We were in the wrong lane.

"Tim!" I shouted, "You ARE on the wrong side of the highway!" It was one of those two-lane highways—one lane northbound and one lane southbound, with a very faded double yellow line between them.

"SWERVE!" I shouted.

At the last second Tim swerved into the safety of our lane. The other car sped by us with its horn blaring. Tim apologized.

"Are you okay? I asked. "You must be very tired. Pull over. I can drive; your dad will never know. I slept. You haven't."

Tim said, "No, I'm okay now. Go back to sleep."

I knew Tim enough to know that arguing would not help. He was stubborn that way, but that stubbornness was also the source of his inner drive, which had helped keep the two of us alive the night before. I trusted him, and went back into a dreamless sleep.

The next time I awoke was to the sound of a Royal Canadian Mounted Police constable's siren roaring up behind us, with its cop car lights flashing. I opened my eyes to see the last of a small town's center fly past us—houses in a row, all with snowy yards. It was just after dark when Tim pulled over to the edge of the road, stopped the car, and rolled down his window. The Mountie told us sternly that we had sped through his town going thirty kilometers per hour (about nineteen miles per hour) over the speed limit. Tim had not even seen the town, he said, and apologized. The Mountie admitted that it was a very small town, one of the do-not-blink towns that you may miss even as you drive through. We had missed it.

The Mountie said, "May I have your license, registration, and insurance card, please?"

Tim took out his wallet as I fished in the glove box for the registration and insurance card that were neatly organized in a folder and handed them to Tim. Tim handed the three items to the Mountie. The Mountie was quiet as he looked over the documents.

He said, "You're Americans. We've had bad experiences with Americans after we ticket them. They say they will pay when they get home, but once they cross the border, they never do. I'm going to give you a speeding ticket, and you have to pay for it right now—right here and right now. Wait for me."

The Mountie turned around and walked back to his cruiser. Tim rolled up the window because it was cold outside. We talked about the ticket. We did not know how much it was going to be, but we did not have much money on us, only enough to pay for gas to get back to Bozeman and to buy a pizza for dinner. We decided that we would take the ticket with us, and the Mountie would just have to trust us. Tim was watching in the rearview mirror and saw him get out of his cruiser.

"Here he comes," Tim said, and he rolled down his window again. The Mountie handed him the ticket. Tim looked at it and showed it to me.

Tim said, "We're not going to pay this now. We can't pay for it now. You'll have to trust us. We have just enough money on us to pay for gas to get home. We promise to pay it. My dad will pay it."

The Mountie said, "No. You pay for this ticket right now. We don't trust Americans."

Tim said, "We can't pay now. We won't pay."

I leaned over Tim and agreed, saying, "Please. We had a terrible, terrible night last night. Can't you give us a break? We promise to pay. It's just, like Tim said, we can't pay now if we want to get home. We do not have enough money."

The Mountie's face hardened as he ordered, "Take the keys out of the ignition. Close the windows, and both of you get out of the car, slowly, with your hands where I can see them."

We did as he ordered. We wondered what was going on and asked him when we were out of the car. He said, "You are both under arrest for speeding and for refusing to pay the fine. I'm taking you back into town. No questions. Lock your vehicle. Get into the backseat of my car."

We walked toward his cruiser; he followed, walking closely behind us. Tim opened the door and we got into the backseat as the Mountie held on to the car door. He put his hand on my head as I got in, pushed me down a little, then closed the door behind us. I tried the handle. There was no door handle. There were no handles for the windows either. And there was a wire cage between the front seat and the backseat. We started to talk to the Mountie when he got in the car, but he ordered us to be quiet. We shut our mouths. It was a short ride back into the sleeping small town. He radioed ahead saying that he was bringing us in.

What had we gotten ourselves into now? He parked next to a snowbank outside of a well-lit municipal building, got out, and let us out. He marched us inside the constable's station in front of him, through the front office, passing the officer on desk duty who nodded knowingly to our Mountie, gave him a key, and glared at us. He then marched us into the back room, where he unlocked the barred cell and ordered us inside. We were scared and hesitated. "Get in!" he ordered. We went in, and he shut the cell door behind us. It locked with a metallic click and the turn of the key that the deskman had handed him.

He said to us, "Now is the time to talk. I arrested you two because you refused to pay your legal fine. We've had trouble with Americans not paying their fines. We're not letting you go until you pay. It's as simple as that. You talk about it while I go get a cup of coffee."

He walked away, and we were alone. I do not remember how much the ticket was for, but Tim still had it in his hands. We looked at it, read it over. We did not have enough money to pay the ticket, period.

Tim and I both carried our money in two places. It is a trick many travelers use. We each had a wallet with cash, and we each had emergency cash stashed away inside our smelly hiking boots—just in case we were robbed. Alone in the cell, we opened our wallets, pulled out our cash, and pooled it. It was not much, maybe twenty or thirty American dollars. We called out to the Mountie, and he walked back to us, sipping his coffee. We showed him the cash we had, emptied our pockets, and showed him our empty wallets. "It's all we have between us," we lied. The Mountie told Tim to hand him the cash, and then he counted it. "It's not enough," he said, "but it'll have to do."

He unlocked the cell and let us out, and offered us coffee, which we politely accepted, even though I did not drink coffee at the time. "I'll drive you back to your car, boys," he said. He was all smiles and friendliness now. It was a quiet ride back. As he let us out of his cruiser, he said, "Drive slowly and stay out of trouble, boys."

"Yes, sir," we said in unison.

I dumped out my coffee in the snow outside Tim's car, and we drove on. By the time we got to Calgary we were hungry, so we pulled off into that shining light of a city. After calculating money for gas and food, we figured we had enough boot cash between us to eat a cheese pizza for supper and just about get back to Bozeman. So we pulled into the first pizza joint we saw and ate hungrily at a Formica-covered table under neon lights. It was a noisy place and a harsh culture clash for us. Tim was talkative. I was not.

Our encounter with the Royal Canadian Mounted Police had not fazed me. I was deeply, emotionally disturbed by our extreme ice climbing adventure, and becoming ever more so, troubled and confused to the depth of my spirit by my encounter with heaven and God. I had thought that maybe, when I woke up, the feeling of being in two places at once might go away. It had not. It haunted me. I was pensive and quiet. Tim tried to cajole me back to my good humor by saying all was well because we had won; we had beat the mountain. He commented on the culture shock of the quiet wilderness compared to the bright lights of the big city. He said he was sorry about being in the wrong lane and about our police encounter. I said it was okay. I was overwhelmed and reeling but could not explain why. I did not smile. I could not talk. Tim tried, but eventually, over our pizza, he gave up and left me alone.

⌒ 21 ⌒

Wrecked

Back in the car, I fell asleep again. When I awoke, we were still on that two-lane highway, headed south in the dark. I looked ahead and again saw a pair of white headlights headed straight toward us, about a half-mile away. Other than the car lights headed directly at us, the road was empty.

Calmly, I said, "Tim, you are on the wrong side of the road again."

"I am not," he said. "You just woke up. You don't know what you are talking about. We are doing fine. I am right where I am supposed to be. Go back to sleep."

"Tim," I insisted, "You're on the wrong side! You're in the wrong lane!"

"I am not!" he said. "Go back to sleep!"

I thought he was wrong, and rather than argue and risk our lives again with a head-on collision, I reached out with my left hand and grabbed the wheel.

Tim looked over at me with his eyes wide. "NO! Stop!" he shouted.

I did not listen to him and instead I jerked down on the steering wheel, forcing the car to the right.

Tim screamed at me, "Noooo!"

Tim was right, and I was not in my right mind. The car leaped to the right and into the emergency lane. I felt the tires on my side hit the gravel just above the edge of the roadside ditch. It felt like the car went up on the two wheels of its passenger side, and maybe it did, just a little. Tim was screaming at me, "What have you done?!" I was screaming, too.

Time slowed down. All the objects in the car drifted past me in a sort of suspended animation—a book, two or three cassette tapes, a crunched up bag, a pencil.

Tim jerked the wheel to the left to compensate. We rocketed to the left, across the centerline, this time seemingly landing on the two wheels on the driver's side. The car was strangely tipped and lurching and completely out of control. I watched as the headlights and front end of an eighteen-wheeler materialized directly in front of us, only feet away, aimed directly at us. Our car and the truck were both doing fifty-five miles an hour. The objects in the air seemed to almost freeze in space. Tim and I kept screaming. Tim saw the truck and jerked the wheel too hard to the right.

He shouted out, "My dad is going to kill me if we wreck the car!"

We missed the front end of the semi by inches. In those few moments, I plainly saw my entire life flash before my eyes, just like they say it does—like a movie. It was superfast and very clear, starting when I was a baby and running right through my entire life, day by day. It was completely unlike what I experienced the night before when I was in hell. This was like watching a reel of my life with sound, flashing rapidly across my inner vision. It blocked out my view of what was actually happening around me inside and outside of the car. It was complete, and yet also extremely fast, brief.

Tim jerked the wheel back to the left because he had overcompensated to the right, or maybe the car was somehow caught on its right side wheels and jerked itself back to the left—because we were about to crash over the side and into the ditch. We swung to the left and hit hard, front-end first on my side against the skidding double rear wheels of the flatbed of the semi.

We hit at an angle in a horrendously violent crash. There was a loud squeal of the semi's locked up and smoking wheels. We both jerked forward hard against our seat belts. Tim hit the steering wheel with his head. I watched the double wheels crush and explode the front end of Tim's car. Metal and plastic went flying. I watched through the windshield, sure that I was about to die and afraid of the pain that was coming, as the steel of the flatbed came at my head even as I helplessly felt it swing forward and hit the dashboard.

Our seat belts locked up. Mine stopped me from flying from my seat through the windshield, where I surely would have crushed my skull against the edge of the flatbed steel that stopped only inches from the other side of the windshield. My head bounced off the dashboard. And then everything stopped.

It was silent. We were still. The front end of the car was completely destroyed, shredded. Parts fell off as we sat there. I stared at the steel edge of the flatbed just on the other side of the windshield. The car's engine was mangled; it had absorbed most of the shock of the impact. Miraculously, Tim and I were pretty much unhurt. I had bruised my chest and whipped my neck but seemed otherwise okay. Then Tim exploded in anger. He started shouting all sorts of expletives at me, screaming that his dad was going to kill him because his car was wrecked. Tim was right, of course. I had wrecked his car.

"Tell your dad that it was my fault. I'll tell your dad because it was my fault," I said.

"Just shut up, Peter," he said.

The truck driver was pounding his fist on the roof of the car, shouting at us, asking if anyone was hurt. We both got out of the car on the driver's side because I could not open the passenger door—it was destroyed. We stood around as the truck driver shouted at both of us, but mostly at Tim, because he thought it was Tim's fault, and from his own fear and anger that he might have killed us. He was shaking, and so were we.

"It was my fault," I stuttered. "I grabbed the wheel. Tim didn't do it. I did. I was asleep and I woke up confused and I grabbed the wheel and I jerked it down."

Pointing at me, the trucker asked Tim, "Is he telling the truth?"

"Yes, he is," said Tim.

"It was my fault," I repeated, and stood there humiliated by what I had done.

After a few minutes, a Canadian Mountie arrived with lights flashing and sorted out what had happened. Traffic was backing up in that rural stretch of highway. The semi was in its lane headed north, and Tim's car was stopped across the southbound lane. Together, both vehicles blocked the entire road. After hearing from the trucker, Tim, and me about what had happened, the Mountie ordered us to try to push Tim's car off the truck, back across the road, and onto the shoulder, so that traffic could get moving again. I went under the flatbed to push from the front end; Tim and the truck driver pushed from over by the driver's door as the Mountie stood on duty surveying the scene and stopping traffic.

It was dark underneath the flatbed, and the Mountie was in a hurry to get us to move the car. He shouted at us in an angry voice, "Push that car out of the way." It was cold out. I was a mental and emotional mess by this point. I blindly put my hand on what was left of the hood of the car without thinking there might be sharp edges or broken glass, or that I should have been wearing gloves. We pushed hard together. The fleshy part of my right hand, between my thumb and palm, sunk into a sharp edge of metal. I felt it cut me, deeply, but I kept pushing anyway and I let it hurt. I had this idea that I deserved the pain and the wound and the blood for having wrecked Tim's car, and for having nearly killed us in a violent wreck.

The car rolled off rather easily from the highway and onto the gravel shoulder. The trucker kept repeating, "Thank you God, thank you God, that nobody died, or got badly hurt, and that my semi was undamaged."

"My dad's going to kill me," Tim said, looking right at me. And then he stopped talking. He was livid, and he was right. The wreck was my fault, and his dad was going to be very angry with him. I felt like a jerk. We were both pretty shaken up, especially considering everything that had happened in the last twenty-four hours. The Mountie got all the legal information he needed— license, registration, insurance, and listened to our story of the crash and why we were in Canada. He did seem to care when I stuttered again and again, "It wasn't his fault. It was my fault. I did this."

He asked us, "What are you going to do now? Where are you going to sleep?"

We didn't know. "It's a clear night," I said. "We have a tent. Can we set it up over there?" I pointed to the side of the road. "We can roll out our sleeping pads and bags off of the side of the highway, sleep there for the rest of the night, and figure out what to do in the morning."

"No, that's a bad idea," he said. "There is a small hotel in town. Get all of your gear and everything you may ever want out of the car. Clean it out. It's a total wreck. It will never drive again." We cleaned out the car.

By this time, a second Mountie had arrived and was directing traffic around the accident scene. The first Mountie opened the trunk of his car for us to load our gear. He continued talking to Tim and the trucker. The temperature was dropping, and I was shaking and shivering. Tim told the Mountie that we did not have enough money to pay for a room in a hotel. The Mountie said, "I don't care if you have any money or not, because no matter what you will not sleep next to the highway." He insisted that he would drive us to the hotel, adding that if we had any other ideas besides going to the hotel that he would arrest us and lock us up. That settled it. We had already spent time that night in a Canadian jail and did not want a repeat event. Neither of us told the Mountie that we'd already visited a cell that night.

I finished cleaning out Tim's car and loading our backpacks, tent, skis and poles, axes, rope, a dozen ice screws, assorted carabiners, and nylon webbing into the trunk of the Mountie's cruiser. I also collected all of Tim's valuables from inside the car—his cassette tapes, a book, and other things, plus all the stuff from his glove box. I felt like I owed it to Tim to do the cleaning. Then, for the second time that night, we climbed into the backseat of a police car. Once more, we were locked in the backseat of a police car, side by side. He drove us to the hotel. It was a silent and short ride, just a couple miles. My hand was bleeding and pulsed with pain from the cut I got when we pushed the car off the road. I said nothing about it and applied direct pressure to stop the blood, wrapping it with my bandana to try to keep my blood off of the car upholstery. I figured that I deserved it.

⪻ 22 ⪼

Beggars

It was probably after midnight when we walked into the hotel lobby. A log fire was burning in the lobby, and there was red wall-to-wall carpet covering the floor. Behind the dark wood check-in counter the hotel manager eyed us suspiciously as we walked in, looking like exactly what we were at that point: two scared and dirty mountaineers. Our backpacks towered behind our heads and axes and rope hung over our shoulders. There were other people in the lobby, and they watched us and assessed us silently. We had stopped for a moment outside of the hotel to stick our cross-country skis and poles into a snowbank outside the front door. The Mountie told us that they would be safe there because it was a crime-free town.

I had the immediate impression that it was a decent hotel, and that unwashed, longhaired, backpack-carrying hippies with cross-country skis were not welcome. Tim and I shed our packs by the door and approached the desk. The couple of guests who loitered in the small and homey lobby backed away from us. We told the manager that we had just totaled—that is, I had just totaled—Tim's car, and that the Mountie who was with us had ordered us to come to the hotel even though we didn't have any money to pay for a room.

"No money, no room," the manager said. "You can leave. Get out. You're disrupting our lobby and disturbing our guests. Please leave right now."

"Mister," Tim begged, "this Mountie is going to arrest us if we leave. He told us so. He'll put us in jail as vagrants if you do not let us stay here for the night. Peter totaled my car, and we have nowhere to go. Please let us stay here."

"I don't care what happens to you," the manager replied. "What's that to me? You'll need to pay to stay here or get out. We're a hotel; we're not a charity. On second thought, just get out of here now!" He pointed to the door.

We looked at the stern-eyed Mountie who had his arms crossed over his chest. He did not look happy. Tim and I looked at each other, and Tim begged again, "Please, we just went through a frightening car wreck, and last night we nearly died of exposure while ice climbing up near Jasper. We need your help. We're college students from Bozeman."

"I don't care what happened to you, who you are, or where you are from; get out," he said.

The guests watched and listened to our little drama. I think they were sympathetic. I pleaded, "J-j-j-just let us u-u-unroll our s-s-s-sleeping bags over b-by the fireplace on the f-f-loor and let us spend the night. We p-prom-ise to be up b-b-before daylight and out the d-d-door b-before your guests are up in the m-m-morning."

The hotel manager chuckled at my stutter and said he had had enough of us. "GET. OUT," he said once more.

Thus, our negotiations with the manager were over, and we resigned ourselves to being arrested for the second time that night. We turned away from the check-in counter and walked toward our backpacks. We both looked at the Mountie in his red uniform, high leather boots, leather belt, and leather shoulder strap. He had been leaning against the wall near the front door, watching and listening. He removed his wide-brimmed hat, held it in his hand, and then he took a step toward us.

This is it, I thought. *Jail*. I was expecting arrest when he spoke up and said to the hotel manager, "John, I think these are good boys who have had a lot of trouble last night and again tonight. This one wrecked the car and he wasn't even driving. Why don't you just let them sleep on the lobby floor tonight, as a favor to me? I'm sure they will be out at the crack of dawn. Right, boys?"

We nodded yes.

"If they're not," he continues, "you call me. I'll still be on duty, and I'll come get them and arrest them. Okay, John? Okay, boys?"

We nodded again and said, "Yes, sir." He handed John his card, and John reluctantly agreed.

"Thank you, sir," we said to the manager scowling at us. We thanked the Mountie too, who gave us a kind grin as he said goodnight. "Get some rest, boys, and don't let me find you here in the morning."

"You won't, sir," Tim said, and I nodded in agreement. The Mountie then turned and left us there.

We ignored the other guests as we unstuffed our sleeping bags, rolled out our sleeping pads close to the fireplace, and without changing clothes slipped into our sleeping bags, side by side, and fell immediately into an exhausted sleep.

The next morning we woke at dawn because the hotel manager made sure of it. "Get up, you two," he snarled. We got up, packed up our gear, shouldered our packs, and thanked him. He grunted and looked away.

Tim asked him if there was a bus station and a bus that was headed south.

"A bus? I thought you said you had no money? You hippies. There's a bus headed south this morning, but it costs money, and you don't have any money. I'm sure they won't let you on the bus for nothing. It will stop just up the road in about an hour outside a shop."

For some reason, maybe it was the look on our faces, the manager's face softened a bit and he handed Tim a bus schedule. We thanked him again, stuffed our sleeping bags, rolled up our pads, packed them away, shouldered all our gear, and went out into the cold, rosy dawn. We stopped to strap our skis and poles to each other's back-packs in a helpful way, and I could tell that Tim, while still angry with me, still liked me enough to be helpful.

The town was quiet and pretty. The night before, after the wreck, we had had no idea where we were, what town we were in, or what the town looked like. It was situated just off the highway, on a parallel side road, which probably had been the main road before the high-way was built. On the far north end of town stood a tall grain silo. We were in farm country. There were a few well-painted houses set closely together, some shops, and a grocery market. There weren't any cars on the road or on the highway. The bus stop was indeed outside one of the small shops. Tim and I stood in the hotel parking lot looking around and talked about what to do next.

It was then that I discovered I had developed a strong stutter. When I was talking to the Mountie and the manager the night before, I had figured that my new stutter was temporary, a result of my nerves, and would be gone in the morning. Instead, every sentence I uttered I stammered. Tim was annoyed. I could see it in his face, and I was shocked.

"W-w-what the . . . ?" I said. I had never stuttered in all my life, not once. I stammered my way through our conversation as we looked at the bus schedule, reviewed our options, and measured our money. We had lied a little to the Mountie and to the manager. We had stashed some of our cash inside our boots. I was feeling humble, embarrassed, and ashamed for having wrecked Tim's car.

"Tim," I stammered, "I am so sorry for what I did. I know your dad is going to be so angry. You tell him it was my fault. You tell him that. If he wants to talk to me, I'll tell him that too."

Tim just shook his head slowly, and looking at the bus schedule, said, "There's a bus leaving in an hour. It looks like it will go right through to Bozeman with a few stops along the way."

"You take the bus. I wrecked your car."

We pooled our money. All together it was enough to get one of us back to Bozeman.

"You take the bus. I'll hitchhike." I had been hitchhiking since high school. My Catholic prep school had been two towns west of my city, and on occasion I'd miss the bus home and have to hitchhike. This practice eventually led me to hitchhiking between UMass and my home, and then up into the mountains of western Massachusetts, New Hampshire, Vermont, Maine, Montana, and Wyoming for backpacking and hiking trips. I was an old hand at hitching rides.

I stuttered out, "I'll be s-s-safe enough."

Tim eyed me curiously, and kindly, and then said, "Let's split the gear."

We split the gear between us, with Tim taking the large and clunky items: four skis, four ski poles, two ice axes, dozens of ice screws, and his ice hammer. We had already divided the tent parts between us. I took our climbing rope, one axe, my two hammers, my stove, and the rest of my gear.

"I'll need to make a hitchhiking sign," I stuttered, and I walked back into the hotel and stammered to the manager, "Pretty please, may I have a piece of cardboard on which to write 'Bozeman,' and may I also borrow a marker with which to write it?"

He smiled knowingly, almost kindly, and handed me a thick black marker and a piece of cardboard that he retrieved from a back room. I wrote Bozeman, MT in big, bold black letters on the cardboard, thanked him again, and walked outside to join Tim.

We chatted a little about his bus route, and I discovered that when I stuttered, if I stopped talking and started over, I stuttered less.

Tim said, "I am unbelievably angry with you for wrecking my car. My dad told me not to let anyone ever drive it and I didn't and now what am I going to say to him? He spent a lot of money on that car. He trusted me. He is going to kill me."

I repeated, "I'm sorry. It was my fault."

Tim said, "After this, when this is all over, I don't ever want to see you again."

I understood why. My time in my own hell gave me a clear understanding of how much pain I'd caused him. I was feeling heartily sorry. Meanwhile, I was still deeply confused and struggling with being a human being, being inside a body, having a brain, and having fingers and toes and a nose and cheeks that hurt from frostbite. I was lost. I did not understand what had happened to me on that ice face. Internally, I was trying to negotiate this world that I found myself in. I knew I was not from here, but where was it I had gone? What was that place? Was it real?

I felt as if I were standing in two worlds at once; one foot here, one foot there, one foot on earth and one foot in heaven. My mind would not focus. This world of blood and bone and sunrise and Tim—all were ugly and not right. Where had I been? What was I? What was this place, this world? I did not belong here. I was not from here. This was not my world. What had happened to me? Who was I? What was I? Where was I? Heaven, that other place that was no place, was where I knew I belonged, was where I was from and wanted to go back to. My soul was on fire, leaping from my body, disconnected from my body, and attached to the other side. I was lost. This world felt completely unreal. Heaven had felt Real. It was the only Real. Only God was Real. I was not even real—at least, my body and brain were not real. Only my soul was real, and it belonged to God, was made by God—I didn't even own my soul anymore. Heaven felt as if it was the only Real.

I craved the love I had felt there. I missed God. I missed the beauty. I had been in paradise, in bliss, in heaven and wholeness, and healing and love and beauty. What had it meant when God said, *You won't live your life?* Maybe now I was getting it: I was not living my life. My life was gone. I felt alien. I felt other. It was as if my vision was split in two—between this world and the world beyond. It felt as if I had two eyes—an inner eye that only saw a drop, a touch, a taste of what I had lost when I chose to come back here, and that drop, that touch, that taste was all I wanted. I regretted my choice to return to my family, to my mom and dad, to return to this earth, to this world, and to my body. What had I done? I had made a mistake. I should never have come back. Why had I come back? I silently said my first prayer to God: *Take me back. Take me Home. I made a mistake. Take me Home now, please.*

God did not grant me my request.

Little did I know that prayer would become my daily prayer for decades. My feeling of being an alien and feeling split between two worlds would remain my experience of reality forever. I was shattered emotionally, spiritually, psychologically. Was it any wonder that my traumas had resulted in a stutter?

Meanwhile, back at the bus stop, Tim had been speaking to me. "Why aren't you listening to me? I said that when I get back to Bozeman I will leave your skis and poles on the front porch of the Men's Co-op. And please, Peter, after you get back, just leave my gear in a corner on the porch for me to find. I'll pick it up at some point. I don't want to see you again. Good luck hitchhiking." We shook hands and parted in a strangely friendly, trusting, and yet broken way.

⮯ 23 ⮰

Not My Body

I turned and walked north toward the highway access road that was a half mile away. It was a beautiful dawn. A rosy-colored sky edging its way to blue brightened above me. I stopped to watch the sky for a time before continuing on and pondered how plain it all was. How uninspiring, how coarse, unrefined, and repulsive even the beauty of a sunrise now seemed compared with the utter and unspeakable Beauty of God. Inside me, the beauty of heaven was real. Even though I could no longer fully feel it within me, I remembered the beauty and love clearly. The memory was so strong, so vivid, that it and the sense of heaven inside me would color my vision of this world for decades to come.

Years later, it struck me: How could it be that I remember any of this? When I was dead, I did not have a body or brain. Without a brain, how could I remember anything of the experience? Aren't memories stored in cells inside the human brain? The only explanation I can think of is that my consciousness, my soul-self (which is my Real self) has a memory that is separate from my body's brain and memory. Somehow my soul interacted and interacts with my body and brain, causing me to remember a soul-memory.

That morning a heavy snow cover of a couple feet blanketed the ground. The main street, the sidewalk on which I walked, and the highway had been plowed clear. There was no wind; all was still. I walked through the quiet town, passing the grain silo on my left. A car went by. The driver stared at me as if I was an oddity, which I guess I was. My long hair stuck out from under my gray wool cap. My orange backpack was packed full and festooned with our blue climbing rope and ice axes. I am sure the look on my face must have been the oddest part of me if it, or any of what I felt inside, showed at all. I felt lost, bewildered, upset, sad, angry; and yet, some of the light that was not (and is not) mine must have been glowing within me, and shining out of my eyes. Over the years, many people have commented on my eyes, saying that they see light in them. That may be true; but, if it is there, it is not mine.

On the snowy shoulder of the highway, I took off my backpack, leaned it against the snowbank, held up my cardboard sign that said BOZEMAN, MT, and waited. As I said before, I was a veteran hitchhiker. Truth be told, the first time I hitchhiked was because I had detention after school for mouthing off to one of the Xaverian Brothers at my all-boys Catholic high school and had missed the bus home. I hitchhiked that day just so I didn't have to call my parents for a ride and tell them I'd had detention.

On that afternoon in 1973, at the age of fourteen, I picked up my heavy St. John's book bag, adjusted my necktie, stood by the side of the road next to St. John's

High School, then hitched the fourteen miles through three towns to my home. Over the years since that detention day, I would often get rides with World War II veterans with their eternally flat-topped haircuts. They would pick up a longhair like me because of hitchhiking karma. They all told me tales of getting back to the States aboard a warship, either from the European or Japanese Theater, and then hitchhiking across America to get back home to their moms, wives, or girlfriends. Those vets told me they felt a duty to other hitchhikers that they needed to repay a debt they felt they owed. It was from one of those fellows that I learned the useful trick of using a piece of cardboard as a hitchhiking sign and to write my destination on it—or, better yet, to write "Home to Mom" on it. A sign had always worked better than my thumb. "Home to Mom" always worked, too, but only if I was actually going home to see my mom. Now, I held up my "Bozeman, MT" sign, sighed, and waited.

But my mind kept up that whirling: *Who am I? What am I doing here? Where am I? What am I? Was it real? Was I real? Did I die? Am I alive? Did this really happen? What is reality? Am I crazy? Can I tell anybody that I died?*

I tried saying, "I died, and I am alive again" out loud. It sounded nuts to me. If it sounded nuts to me, and I was the one who had experienced it, it would definitely sound crazy to most anyone I told. They'd think, *This dude is bonkers!* So, standing there on the shoulder of the highway in the morning light, I decided right then to never say a word about it. I would never tell my tale.

Who would believe me, anyway? Who had even heard of a near-death experience in 1980? I had never heard of such a thing and had no idea how to explain what had happened to me. Besides, I did not think about it as near death. There was nothing near about it. It was death. I had died. I had been taken. I had been "near" death once before when I was about eight years old. I was drowning in a river, and I went under for what I believed was the last time. I felt myself blacking out. Just then, I was pulled out of the river by the strong arms of an unknown man. That was "near" death. I could have died, but I did not die in that river.

I died when I was twenty-one, but I did not start using the common term—near-death experience—until many years later. On the day after our car wreck with that eighteen-wheeler in Canada, I had no cultural or historic or literary reference points about what dying was actually like. I had read nothing about it. All the people I knew who died had stayed dead. Not one had come back. As a boy, I had been to plenty of wakes with my Dad and had seen enough dead people to know what death looked like from the outside. But what did death look like from the inside? Other than my experience two nights before, I had no idea.

The only thing I knew about dying and coming back came from the Bible, from the Gospels about Jesus and Lazarus. Jesus prayed to God, then called out to Lazarus, "Lazarus, come out!" The dead man came out wrapped in his death shroud. That is all I knew about what we now call near-death experience. I knew Lazarus had died and had come back. If Lazarus had anything to say about it, it was never written down.

Over and over again for many months to come I repeated those questions to myself: Who am I? What am I? Where am I? What is God? Where is God? How can I feel like I am in two places at once, with a part of me in heaven and part of me on earth? Part of my problem was that when I was dead I had known the answers to each of these questions; moreover, I had known the answers to a great many more questions—questions I hadn't even known I'd had. I had known so much more when I was dead. Truths had been revealed to me, but ever since I'd come back into this world, I could not and still cannot remember any of the answers. I know only that I had known, that I no longer knew, and that I might not know again until I died again. It was frustrating.

Hitchhiking to Bozeman, Montana, at dawn that day, I decided I'd never tell anybody about what had happened that night on the Lower Weeping Wall. I'd keep that secret, in part because I did not understand it, in part because I had no words to describe the indescribable, and in part to keep myself from being judged. I was scared that nobody would believe me. Even worse, I feared that if I told my story, people would think that I was really and truly insane. So I would keep my death a secret.

I knew I could keep a secret because I'd been keeping secrets since I was fourteen years old. Because of Andrea, keeping secrets had become normal for me. I could keep my mouth shut, could lock down inside and hide a part of me. I was good at this, and strangely, this skill of secret keeping would become quite useful when I became a pastor. Pastors are secret keepers, or at least they should be. I kept parishioners' secrets and still do; I will always keep the secrets shared with me by my congregants about their personal pain, tribulations, and tragedies. It is a role I handle well.

I decided that morning that I would tell the rest of my story—the snow cave, the climb, the exposure and frostbite, the car wreck—all of it, except for the part about my death. That, I would keep to myself—or, rather, as I discovered, between God and me. Of course, keeping secrets, keeping a part of oneself hidden, takes effort and energy, and there is a cost for that.

❦ 24 ❦

Stammering to Bozeman

On the shoulder of the highway I leaned my back-pack against my legs and held my sign up as cars and trucks whizzed by me. The day was beautiful, yet it did not seem beautiful to me. The entire world looked flat and uninspired since I returned to this life. Beauty seemed ugly and drab, sort of two-dimensional and cartoon-like. Compared to the beauty of heaven, everything was just less-than. I was reeling inside, still feeling displaced, disassociated, and disoriented, when a red Fiat, a two-seater convertible, pulled over just beyond where I was standing, and tooted. I shouldered my backpack and hurried over. The driver leaned across the passenger seat and rolled down the window. He said he could take me across the border and all the way to Missoula, Montana.

I stuttered, "Gr-gr-great."

The driver said, "I think we can fit your pack in the trunk if I put my suitcase behind the seats." He got out to open his small trunk, and moved his suitcase into the small space behind the front seats. I put my backpack into the trunk, closed it, and got into the car. Holding out his hand, he introduced himself as a professor from the University of Montana in Missoula.

"I'm Pe-Peter," I stuttered, "I go to MSU in Bozeman."

"You look like a student," he laughed. "That's why I picked you up." And off we drove. He chatted about philosophy and history and literature for a while, describing his work, all of which I tried to listen to but have long since forgotten because my mind was all topsy-turvy.

He glanced over at me as he drove, and said, "You look terrible. Are you okay?"

I was silent for a few minutes as I thought about what to say and how to say it. I kept shifting around in my seat, my body twitchy and uncomfortable. He let the silence sit until I slowly told him that I'd awoken that morning with a stutter I'd never had before, coming as a result, I thought, from the car wreck the previous night. It took me a while to say anything at all. I did not like my stutter, and I was trying to come to grips with it, on top of everything else. The professor was patient with me and allowed me to tell my tale, starting with skiing across the frozen lake with Tim a week before, finding the burned-down cabin, the snow cave, the ranger's cabin, the ice climb, the frostbite, the exposure, the falling asleep on the cliff, our self-rescue, the jail cell, the car wreck, and the hotel. I told him the whole tale minus the crazy part about my death and dying, hell and heaven, God and Love, and about how coming back to this now-unreal world left me feeling completely undone.

I discovered that I was able to tell my story about the ice climb and the car wreck without telling the whole of it. I was able to keep out the most important part. I had a new secret. But deep inside me a pressure was starting to build to speak about what had happened—I could feel it. I found out that morning that I was going to have to battle with it, this thing that wanted and demanded to be spoken aloud even though I never wanted to speak of it for fear of ridicule. I was an expert at compartmentalization, and I would win, or so I believed.

The professor listened to my entire story without interruption, and then we drove a long way in silence as I stared out the window at the passing scenery and tried to get a grip on myself.

The professor interrupted the silence. "We need a plan to cross the border into the States."

"Why?" I asked.

He said something about having crossed into Canada alone, and that the border guards might have questions about his having a young man with him. He was kind and considerate and had a good heart, and I could see the Light of God reflected in him; I felt it in him. He was the first person in whom I saw the Light of God reflected so clearly and so obviously, and he would not be the last. The Light was so plain to see I wondered that I had never seen it before. His eyes shined and I felt the Light, the Love, radiating from him. I was even more amazed that he seemed completely unaware of it. As they say, the eyes are the windows to the soul. In the years since that day, and through my practices of prayer and meditation, I have come to the place where if I place my hand near the hands of another person, or over their hearts or back, I can feel the radiance of their souls with my soul. It feels like a hum in the palm of my hand, or like a radiant warmth. The professor seemed heaven-sent.

He said, "We'll get off this main highway and start taking smaller highways as soon as we can. We'll have an easier time of it at a smaller crossing that I know." He handed me his road map. "You'll have to navigate. You're a backpacker so I assume that you can read maps. Can you?"

"Yes, I can," I said.

"Good. The crossing is a little out of the way." At the next exit, we pulled off and then he pulled over, took the map back, and flipped through the pages. "This one," he said, pointing to a road and a marked crossing on the map. "Find us our best route."

"Okay. Let's go. I'll n-n-navigate," I stuttered. And off we went. It was a quiet ride, as there wasn't much that I could say aloud. Lots of things were running through my head, and the distraction of navigation was welcome. An hour or more later, we approached the border.

"Are you ready?" he asked.

"I am," I said.

We stopped at what was obviously a lonely outpost for the border guard and rolled down our windows. Two border guards heard our story. "Get out of the car," one ordered, "and go wait inside our waiting room. Leave the keys in the car."

We did as ordered and watched them search the car. They searched it rather thoroughly—under the seats, inside his suitcase, and in the trunk. When they opened the trunk and saw my backpack with all my climbing gear, they came to get us. "You're all set," one guard said, adding, "Welcome home." We smiled and thanked them, then drove across the border and into the small town of Sunburst, Montana.

More hours passed as we headed south. We said little and only stopped for fuel along the way. I refused his offer to buy me food. I was fine, I said—I lied. He had already been so kind to me that I could not accept his offer of food, too. I slept some as we drove toward

Missoula, and when I awoke, he entertained me with his stories and cassettes.

Just outside Missoula, the professor pulled over to the side of the highway near the off-ramp. He invited me to his home for dinner, promising that he would get me back on the highway the next morning after a meal, a shower (I really needed a shower after more than a week without one), and a good night's sleep. I thanked him but gently refused. It was not the first time a kind Montanan had offered to let me spend the night in their home. I stuttered, "Good-bye, and thank you for your kindness." Whoever he was, for I have long since forgotten his name, I thank God for him.

☞ 25 ☜

Kind Cowboy

I walked a distance along US Route 90 southbound, positioned myself on the on-ramp, and held up my sign. My next ride, which I do not remember much about, dropped me just north of Butte, Montana, on the highway just before the off-ramp into Butte. That driver drove on into Butte, and I was still headed south. It was late in the afternoon. In those days, the population of Montana was roughly 1.7 persons per square mile, which meant that the state was seriously underpopulated. It was about an hour before the first car drove by, but it was headed into Butte. I waited for hours, watching for a single vehicle headed toward Bozeman. No one, not one, headed south past Butte. Every one of the few cars and trucks that did appear on the highway pulled off and headed into Butte.

I was beside myself, barely holding my mind and self together. Still shattered emotionally, psychologically, and spiritually, I was a wreck, and I wept. The sun had set, and night was falling. I knew I either had to get a ride or I was going to spend the night alone on the side of the road huddled in my sleeping bag and nearly out of my mind. I was determined not to do that, so I repositioned myself just north of the off-ramp into Butte and took out my flashlight. It was a long off-ramp, maybe a couple miles long into Butte. It took another twenty minutes in the fading twilight before I spotted a pair of headlights slowing down for the off-ramp. It was a pickup truck moseying down the highway. I waited until the truck got pretty close, and then, waving my flashlight, I stepped out into the highway into his path, raising my arms above my head. I flagged the driver to stop just inches from my chest. I nodded to him, and he, in his cowboy hat, nodded back. He rolled down his window and asked, "What seems to be the trouble, young man?"

I stuttered, "I'm stuck out here. I was in a bad car wreck up north of Calgary, and I'm trying to get to Bozeman and back to school. If I have to spend the night on the road, I'd rather do it closer in to Butte. Would you be kind enough to give me a ride into Butte?"

He studied my face and said, "Sure, I will. Toss your pack into the back there, and climb on into the cab." So I did. He had the Light in his eyes, too.

He asked me about the wreck. As quickly as I could, I told him with my stutter and a few tears that I struggled to hold back. I told him just about everything, except the parts about my death and hell and heaven, summarizing the whole thing in about ten minutes. He listened patiently, and then said, "Have you eaten?"

"Not since the night before last when I had pizza in Calgary."

"I'm taking you to dinner at a diner then, and I won't take no for an answer," he said. I declined, thanking him for his kindness, but he took me there anyway. Hungry as I was, I accepted his offer when we reached the parking lot. We sat across from each other at a table for two. He told me to order anything I wanted, and so I did. As I ate and talked, he listened and sipped his coffee with cream. He ate nothing.

After I had a slice of pie, which he insisted I have, and with me feeling significantly better, he asked if I intended to hitch to Bozeman that night. Since I was feeling better, I said I did. "Come on," he said, "get in the truck. Let's go." After driving for a bit, we stopped at a bus station.

"I'm buying you a bus ticket to Bozeman," he said. "Your dad would do the same for my son if he found him stuck, hungry, and far from home, and you had better not argue about this."

It makes me tear up to this day when I think about that cowboy. I do not know who he was, but I remember him and thank God for his kindness. I stood next to him at the ticket counter while he made the transaction—a cowboy and a dirty hippie. He handed me my ticket and said I had better call my mother to let her know that I was okay. Before I could say I did not have a dime to make the collect call, he handed me a quarter. I shook his hand and again thanked him for his kindness. I wanted to hug him, but that felt like I was overstepping somehow. He simply smiled and said, "It's a pleasure to meet you, young man. And remember, God loves you."

Wow, I thought, *he must be some kind of angel.* The kindness of strangers has never ceased to amaze me.

The bus station was typical of bus stations everywhere in America in those days: fiberglass benches, a dirty floor tramped with melted snow, weak yellow lighting, and vagabonds like me. A pay phone hung on the wall. I put in my quarter, dialed the operator, and asked if I could place a collect call. My mom answered. The operator said to my mom, "Would you like to accept a collect call from . . ." and to me the operator said, "Say your name." I stuttered out my name. Mom accepted.

"What's wrong?!" she said. "You're stuttering? Are you okay?"

I told my mom through my stutter and tears that I was okay and unhurt, other than a cut on my palm that I had butterflied shut with my first aid kit and had bandaged over, and of course there was my new stutter. I told her about the car wreck, and how I had caused it, and how I had awoken that morning with a stutter. I told her that Tim had taken a bus, that I was hitching, and that a kind cowboy had bought me dinner and a bus ticket to Bozeman from Butte, where I was now in a bus station, and about how he had helped me make this call. I told her I would call her when I got back to the Men's Co-op.

She cried a little, and then put Dad on the phone. He was concerned but glad when I assured him I was okay. I wanted to tell them both what had really happened to me. I wanted to tell them that I had died, gone to heaven, seen them from there, seen God's love for them, had gone through hell, had been forgiven and loved. But I did not have the words to describe what I had experienced— and besides, they were already worried about me and my wild wilderness lifestyle, and they had other worries of their own. I could not tell them. They would think I had finally gone crazy or that I was on drugs. Unformed as my thoughts were, it was still on the tip of my tongue, still wanting to be told, but I stuffed the story down and said nothing about it.

My dad said, "Your mom and I love you. Take care of yourself and call us when you get to Bozeman."

"I will," I said. "I love you, too." We hung up. I was still feeling miserable, but at least I wasn't hungry. and I was grateful to the cowboy, and to my mom and dad, so I found a seat on a fiberglass bench, sat down with my backpack leaning against my legs, hung my head down, and tried to keep myself from crying.

About an hour later the bus to Bozeman arrived. I put my backpack in the luggage compartment under the bus, boarded with all my fellow passengers, and fell asleep. I awoke in Bozeman, got off the bus into the cold night air, shouldered my backpack, and hiked several blocks to the Men's Co-op.

In the living room, a few of the guys were sitting on the overstuffed and tattered chairs and sofa watching TV. They all said hello and asked me how my trip was. I stuttered, "It was great. I'm going to bed." My roommate, Mark, was already in our room, in bed and asleep. He had a fire going in our fireplace. I needed that. I leaned my pack against a clear space along the wall, found my thermal pajamas under my pillow where I had left them the week before, put them on, sat down on my mattress, which was on the floor, tried to pray, and found I could not. I crawled under my covers and watched the fire in the fireplace. Its crackling, sparks, and flames soothed me. I watched the flames for quite a while, and finally, safe and warm in my bed, I drifted off into a dreamless sleep.

∽ 26 ∽

Good-Bye, Tim and the Theater

The next morning, just as I opened the front door and stepped onto the porch to walk to class, Tim walked up the front stairs carrying my cross-country skis and poles. He said nothing as he leaned them gently against the house. "I'll be right out with your gear," I said, and went back inside and downstairs to my room to get his gear that I had piled up before heading to class. Back on the porch, in the chill morning air, I gave him his rope, ice screws, and the part of his tent that I'd carried.

Tim told me that he had telephoned his dad and that his dad and he were both angry with me. Tim then said he did not want to see me again, though that was already likely since I was leaving in a week for a ten-week national theater tour. I apologized to Tim once more and added that our paths would not cross on campus because I was leaving soon. By the time I returned, the trimester would be almost over and he might be gone. We shook hands and even smiled a bit. After all, we had been through quite a lot together.

Tim picked up his gear, slung the rope over his shoulder, looked me in the eye with a mix of anger, friendship, love, and trust, and then walked down the steps. He was headed back the way he had come, toward the university. I sighed and went back inside the co-op to wait a few minutes so that we wouldn't have to walk the same route so closely together.

After the theater tour ended, months later, and I was back in Bozeman for a few days, Tim surprisingly showed up on the Men's Co-op porch one afternoon. I happened to be home at the time, packing to leave for Massachusetts. Tim had come by to say that he had thought a lot about the car wreck, about our climb, and about our week snow caving together. He said that, upon reflection, he had forgiven me for wrecking his car. He had come to understand that, although I was at fault, it had happened because we were both a mess. I thanked him, and to this day I appreciate his forgiveness more than I can say. That was the last I saw or heard of Tim.

The morning Tim left my skis for me on the front porch, I walked alone to my one and only class that trimester. It was in the Communications Department, and the class was called "The Theater of Silence." We had been in rehearsal for a national tour since the autumn of 1979. It was theater for the deaf. During the spring and summer of 1979, back in Massachusetts, I had helped my friends organize and run a Friday night coffeehouse in the basement hall of a Roman Catholic church twenty miles from my home. I performed as a clown. The coffeehouse was packed every Friday night with youth from the surrounding towns and cities. We had a live band, popcorn, poetry, and an open mic. That summer, I had begun clowning just to be part of the entertainment. My makeup and costume were so complete that nobody knew who I was. I kept my identity hidden. That was a delight for me.

When I arrived at Montana State University in the autumn of 1979, I had planned on continuing my English major and adding classes to my as-yet undeclared minor in anthropology. When I got to the Bozeman campus, I did as my college advisor at UMass had advised: I called him to discuss my MSU courses. He told me that I had to take a Shakespeare class for my major that autumn because I would not be able to take it the next year from UMass. I discovered that the Shakespeare class met at the same time as my dream class in Native American anthropology. That anthropology class was part of the reason I had picked MSU in the first place. This left me one course short of a full load.

As often was the case, a cute woman solved my problem for me: she mentioned that she was taking a sign language class in the Communications Department. I thought, *Why not?* and signed up. On the first day of class, the professor and chairman of the Communications Department, Dr. Jack O., told the class that there would be auditions for the Theater of Silence in two weeks. The Theater of Silence was Jack's baby. For the previous ten years, Jack had taken actors on a 24,000-mile, 64-show, spring tour across fourteen western states. The show was performed in American Sign Language and was primarily for deaf audiences. Jack said that the planned 1980 tour would play small towns, big cities, and universities, and include a shakedown tour in Alberta and British Columbia. It was an open audition. Bill, a profoundly deaf pantomime, performed for the class that day along with a couple of actors from the year before. I thought, *Why not? I'm a clown, and I can learn the art of mime from Bill.*

I called my parents that night and asked them what they thought. I had planned to attend Montana State University for just the fall trimester. If I got into the show, I would stay in Montana until June. My parents encouraged me to audition. I worked up a routine with the help of that same cute woman. I auditioned, and to my surprise I was selected. For all of that academic year I was at MSU the actors in the troupe worked with Jack to put together a cabaret-style show with music, dancing, acting, and mime—all in American Sign Language. It turned out that I was a natural at performance and sign language.

When I returned from ice climbing, our troupe had only a week to polish up the show before our scheduled tour was to begin. Before my trip to Canada, I had promised Jack that I would be a driver for the fifteen-passenger van and for the pickup truck that pulled a trailer. The van would transport all the actors and crew; the pickup would haul the large box trailer containing all our costumes, makeup, luggage, stage lights, and sound equipment.

At rehearsal that first day back, I kept my stutter a secret by speaking only in sign language. It was an easy thing to do. We all signed all the time anyway because it would have been impolite to speak with Bill there. Using American Sign Language, I told Jack, the actors, and the crew about the car wreck with the semitrailer, and ended by saying that I was just too shaken up to drive. The other drivers were angry with me, and rightly so, because it would mean more driving and less rest for them. "What can I do?" I stuttered out loud and signed at the same time. "I'm a wreck."

Silence filled the room. Bill asked in sign what everybody was staring at. One of the women signed to Bill and said out loud, "Peter has a stutter. He didn't have a stutter before." Adding to me, "Peter, is your stutter real?" I nodded my head yes as I fought back tears and signed yes with my hand. Nobody knew what to do or what to say until Bill signed with a jerky hand motion, indicating a mimed stutter: "He doesn't stutter in sign. So it won't hurt our performance." That relieved the tension, and everyone laughed. Jack said they would figure out a new driving schedule and that he, and everyone, was glad that I was unhurt. By the time the tour was over I had mastered my stutter enough to get by without showing it too much. My stutter still comes out if I get too upset, anxious, or nervous, though.

The troupe had no idea how messed up I really was. I used the car wreck and my stutter as a wall to hide behind. Nobody asked any more questions of me, not even a "How was your trip?" This was okay by me. I did not want to talk about it. My inner world, unseen by them, and unrevealed by me, was one of dislocation. Every movement of every day had become an interior battle to stay rooted in the world. I was in the gym with these people, talking with them, but half of me was still in heaven—or, rather, it felt like more of me was Over There than standing in the gym with them. I felt constantly on the verge of jumping out of my skin and could barely sit or stand still.

Our president, Susan, called our meeting to order. I lay on the floor and tried to keep still; but before long Susan interrupted the meeting and said, "Peter, I know you're not feeling well, but will you please stop squirming on the floor?" I tried, but my body felt like an itchy wool suit, and I wanted it off. I squirmed, but I tried to keep still. I was moving to keep my sanity, such as it was, in place. The more time that passed, the more difficult being in the world was becoming.

Rhanda and Kerri, both my dear friends and actors in the troupe, gave me hugs. I was glad they did. Their hugs and love grounded me in the world a bit; throughout our theater tour, their friendship and love and our closeness kept me sane. They both knew I had changed somehow, but I never explained why.

Decades later, in Facebook conversations with Kerri, I finally told her what had happened to me and why I had changed so much back then. She replied that, in all her life before then and since, I'd been the only person who taught her about unconditional love. Even in those early days after I died, love seemed to be all I had. I really had nothing else. I'd been stripped of myself somehow, had become empty, and so I clung to love inside of me. I clung to God; I clung to the love of God—and that love apparently clung to me and showed through me. I knew that it was not me. It was not my love; I could not own it or claim it. It simply came through me, and that is all.

I had that feeling of standing in two places at once, with a foot here and a foot there, with one eye seeing here and one eye seeing Over There. It was more than a feeling—it was and is an inner reality for me that has remained unchanged for decades. It is still with me to a large extent, but it is not as disturbing as it was during those first months and years after I died. Since then, I've become more adjusted to the confusing sense that

I'm simultaneously in two places. It feels, in a way, like I am inside the Matrix from the film—only instead of our reality being run by an evil machine, a loving God creates our reality. I know that this world is not the highest reality, but it is one that I can't escape; I'm just here until God takes me Home.

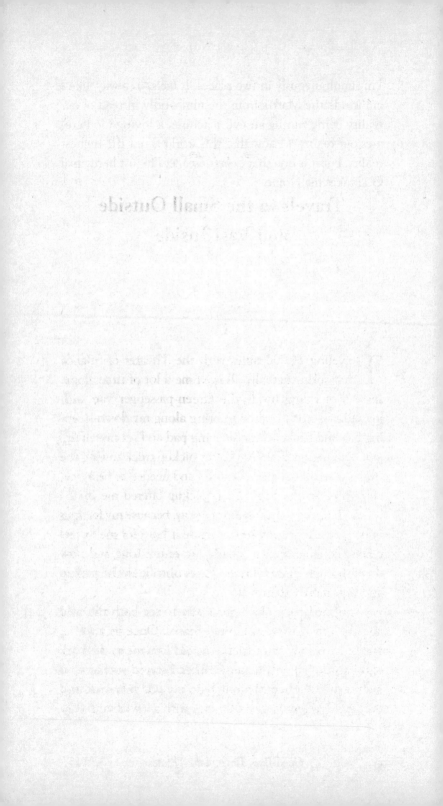

⮐ 27 ⮑

Travels in the Small Outside
and Vast Inside

Traveling 24,000 miles with the Theater of Silence that spring actually allowed me a lot of time alone. Instead of riding inside the fifteen-passenger van with my fellow actors, I opted to bring along my down sleeping bag and backpacking sleeping pad and set myself up, alone, in the back of our theater pickup truck towing the trailer with all our gear. I wanted and needed to be alone, and riding in the back of the pickup offered me that. I was no longer good company anyway, because my feelings of dislocation and my stutter made it hard for me to feel companionable. I spent nearly our entire long and slow drive through those fourteen states outside in the pickup and kept mostly to myself.

It turned out to be a great way to see both the wild and the urban western United States. Once in a while, one or two of my actor-friends would join me in the back of the truck, but only in fair weather. I stayed out there no matter the weather. My long hair, my odd behavior, and my East Coast ways set me at odds with a few of my fellow thespians; it was better that I be alone. Most of the time I had the opportunity to ponder what had happened to me, to meditate, and to pray.

Through reflection and prayer, I discovered that what I wanted most of all was to be dead again, to go back to heaven. I had made a huge mistake; I did not want to be in this world. I was not suicidal, but I wanted and needed to go back to heaven instead of living in this world that seemed so two-dimensional by comparison. The beauty there made everything here—even the vast and varied beauty of the American West—seem plain, flat, and uninspiring. Even so, from the back of the pickup truck I observed many incredible sights: the Rocky Mountains from Montana to Arizona, the Black Hills of South Dakota, Snake River Canyon in Idaho, the desert of New Mexico, Death Valley, the Pacific Ocean, redwood forests, the lush Northwest, huge herds of antelope, incredible sunsets after Mount St. Helens erupted, and every major city in the American West. All of it was stunning to see, but somehow it was simply less, flat somehow, and unappealing. All I wanted was to go Home. Thus, it was in the back of the pickup truck that I began praying.

"God, I made a mistake. I don't want to be here. Take me back. Let me die. Kill me now. Take me home. I don't want to be here. TAKE ME HOME!" This became my new prayer, my daily prayer for decades. It is a prayer and an attitude that is still with me, although during the last several years to a lesser degree.

I had learned meditation when I was a senior at St. John's High School in Shrewsbury, Massachusetts. My senior year religion class teacher had gone on a private retreat to St. Joseph's Abbey, the Trappist monastery in Spencer, Massachusetts, where the monks taught him how to meditate in the traditional contemplative style called centering prayer, or prayer of the heart. My teacher was enthralled by meditation, so one day he pulled down the shades in our classroom, closed the doors, and taught the class what he knew. I was hooked on meditation from that day on and have practiced ever since.

In general, meditation is the practice of quieting the mind, lifting the heart, and listening to God, or listening for God. Meditation in prayer opens the door to stillness and allows me to experience a tiny taste of heaven here on earth. By the time I had died in 1980 I had been practicing meditation for about four years. After I came back, meditation became my lifeline to God, and my stability in this world.

In order to still the mind, those who meditate often repeat a prayer, personalized mantra, or short chant. Back in the summer of 1979, eight months before climbing Lower Weeping Wall, while backpacking in Gallatin National Forest in Montana with my British buddy, Jeremy, and after years of meditative practice, I had finally struck upon what would become my first and second meditation prayer chant. The first was the name *Jesus*, broken into two syllables: *Je* on my in breath and *sus* on my out breath, repeated over and over until the words fell away and one was left only with breath and gentle focus. The second meditation, and the one I still use today, is the Jesus Prayer:

> Lord Jesus Christ, son of God, have mercy on me, a sinner.

The Jesus Prayer, through decades of regular practice, has burned itself deeply into my mind. It plays like an endless tape loop in my subconscious, in the basement of my mind, making it a simple thing nowadays to open the cellar door and let it fill my active thoughts; such is the benefit of long and dedicated practice. My meditative prayer practice has sustained me through the years. But back in the spring of 1980, when I was touring the United States in the back of a pickup truck, I plunged deeply into meditation and prayer because I was desperate for a direct and yet unattainable reconnection to God.

❧ 28 ❧

The Sinner and the Dream

I judged myself poorly. I was guilty, and obviously so. It seemed to me then, as it does now, that sin is causing pain to others. It's that simple. Sin is the hurt we inflict on others, intentionally or unintentionally. This entire world, and by that I mean the entire known universe we live in (and the unknown, for that matter), exists because it has brokenness; without that brokenness, it would not exist.

I also know that God is perfect. God is the only perfect there is. If God alone is perfect, nothing else can be perfect. This world, including all of the known universe and earth, is by nature of its existence imperfect. It exists because of imperfection. If it was perfect, it would not be what it is. If it was perfect, it would be God. That it is imperfect is not wrong or bad or evil. It just is. If it were not imperfect, it would not exist. To exist, this world (meaning the entirety of this universe) must be broken. Sin, it seems to me, is part and parcel of being a human being. To be human is inevitably and unavoidably to cause pain to others, especially those we love. God knows this—at least, God knew this about me.

People often ask me if dying has made me a better person. I think what they mean is, Do I still sin? Do I still hurt people? The answer is, yes, I still hurt people, and I still sin. Oddly, I am pretty much the same person I was before I died, even though the experience changed me radically. I am still, like you, a frail human being. I am still a creature made by God and, therefore, wholly imperfect. I have sinned; I sin, and I dare say, so do you. I am certain I will sin again. I do pray that when I die again God will forgive my sins as before. I pray that my shame upon meeting God again will allow God's love to reign inside me. I believe God will forgive me again: because God is love, and because God told me I could return to the heaven that was within me because of God's love for me.

I am certain that there are many of you who have been unmistakably touched by God. You know it when it happens, and you are irrevocably changed. I simply know that God is Real. I do not have to believe that; I know it. God is Real. God is Real and the only Real there is. I just know now, and have known for decades, that God knows me, thoroughly, through and through, every bit, every word, every thought, every emotion, and every action. Believe me, I have tried my hardest to escape from God. I have run as hard and as far as I could. I did not want this life as I have it. This life came with this bifurcation of me. I am split in two. I wanted to return to my old life. Yet, even as I ran from God, I simultaneously dove into God. I just held part of myself back until God wore me out, until I finally understood that resistance was futile. Why did

I try to run? I was afraid that God would consume me. I was afraid that I would no longer be me. I know it sounds crazy, but I am used to that.

When I could not run any longer, I simply gave myself up to God. So far, I am not consumed.

≈ 29 ≈

Hitching East

Back in 1980, sadness and confusion were my domi-
nant feelings, and that sadness traveled home with
me from Montana to Massachusetts. My best high school
buddy, Steve, had driven westward all the way from Massachusetts in his little red pickup truck to collect me and
my bike, skis, clothes, and gear and take us home to Massachusetts. Just east of Bozeman, Steve's pickup threw a
rod, which killed the engine.

Steve wound up hitchhiking to the Men's Co-op.
We decided that the truck was worthless and we would
just hitchhike home, so I packed all of my stuff in boxes
and mailed it back east. On the day before our departure,
quite suddenly, Steve developed a debilitating sharp pain
in his lower right side. We did not know what it was. I'd
already moved out of my basement room and was sleeping
on a mattress up in the attic. Steve lay down in that attic
room, unable to rise for three or four days and nights. Not
knowing what to do or what the problem was, I fed him
massive doses of vitamin C. After a few days, he felt better. Of course, as you may have suspected, it turned out

to be appendicitis. A week after we got home, he had a relapse and required emergency surgery.

It took four days and nights to hitchhike home. Our first leg was a ride across Montana with a family who took us hours out of their way into Wyoming. They were coming back from a hospital. The young fellow in the backseat had a brand-new plaster cast from his ankle up to his thigh, and he rested his leg across our laps for the eight-hour drive.

At a truck stop in Sheridan, Wyoming, we learned that dozens of hitchhikers had been stuck there for days and days. We walked to the end of the hitchers' line, held up our Home to Mom sign, and had a ride in a semi in less than ten minutes. The other hitchhikers all gave us the evil eye. That truck driver even bought us both dinner at the truck stop. He had a doctorate in philosophy and was a fine conversationalist.

In Nebraska, we had a ride with a speedy driver who had already collected eleven tickets since he'd left Oregon a couple days before. He said he had no intention of paying a single ticket.

In Iowa, our pickup truck driver learned that we had never seen his beautiful state and insisted we take back-country highways so he could show it to us. He was right; Iowa is amazingly beautiful.

In Cleveland, a crazy ice cream truck driver took us on a rush-hour romp ten miles in the wrong direction and left us in the middle of a desolate and gang-ridden urban landscape. It was after dark. We saw that it was dangerous, but we had no choice but to hitch on that perilous road.

The first car that rolled up approached slowly. It was a big, souped-up Buick lowrider blaring Spanish music with all the windows down. Inside were four gang members, all wearing red bandanas tied around their heads. They laughed when they saw us, and one of them asked us what we were doing there. We explained about the crazy ice cream truck driver. They told us that we were in gangland and it was dangerous here for us. We said that we had just figured that out and they laughed. We could see they liked us. They talked amongst themselves in Spanish, and then the man in the passenger seat said that we could get hurt if we stayed there, and thank God they found us first.

They said there was a bus station a couple miles from there, and that we had better go with them if we wanted to stay alive. They offered to drive us to the bus station and opened a car door and popped the trunk. The driver said, "Do you trust us, man?" What choice did we have? It was a dangerous neighborhood. They had guns. I could see one. Steve and I shoved our backpacks into the large backseat and climbed in. Three of them sat up front, and one sat in the back with us. They were nice to us. It took me by surprise. Angels come in all sorts of disguises. It was not the first nor the last time in my life that gang members would be kind to me.

We all laughed and enjoyed our time with them. They drove us to the bus station, and warned us to stay inside, because it was dangerous outside. They waited for us to enter the station, and then waved and laughed as the driver leaned on the horn before they peeled out and sped away. They are probably still telling stories about the crazy gringos they picked up hitchhiking in a bad neighborhood.

We bought a bus ride out of Cleveland to Rochester and eventually landed on the side of the highway hitching east again. We made it to Albany, New York, where we slept the night in our sleeping bags just off the tarmac at the curb at the Albany tollgate.

Our last ride—in a BMW—took us across Massachusetts. The driver was headed to Boston. Ravel's Boléro was playing in his tape deck. It was the day I would learn to love classical music. Our driver kindly dropped us at the front doors of our respective family homes—Steve in Bolton and me in Marlborough. Naturally, I had not told my parents I was hitchhiking home from Montana. They were surprised enough when a BMW pulled up that they came outside to see what was going on. I thanked my driver, who kindly complimented me to my parents.

Being home did not help me clarify things much. My older sister Andrea was still missing. Melissa, her toddler daughter, had been adopted by my parents, and was now my sister. I carried my inner darkness and confusion in silence, hiding it as best I could. I do not know if my mom and dad ever noticed that I'd changed. We never talked about it. If they ever asked, I never said anything, so how would they know? Besides, their world was busy with a new child in the house.

Over the next few months I found myself living more in heaven than on earth. I was in the world but most certainly not of it. Church, religious education, meditation, chanting, and prayer had taught me that God can be found within. So that is where I looked, that is where I went.

The Book of Revelation 3:21–3:22 says, "I stand at the door and knock. Open the door and let me in." The only special and safe and calm space I had was my inner space, my inner world. My inside was the cause of my turmoil, and that leaked into my outside world.

To calm myself, I'd chant in my mind, "Lord Jesus Christ, son of God, have mercy on me, a sinner." Either that or I'd close my eyes and pray myself to stillness, if I could. I had learned to dive inside of myself, as if compelled, as if the only salvation for my sanity was to seek God, and so I continued with that practice back on the East Coast: I isolated myself as best I could by diving inside my mind, breath, and soul.

In Massachusetts, I was less connected to people. I found them confusing because they could not see what I could see—that life was brief, death was always close, the world was an illusion, and only God was real. I could see the light inside people, feel it from them. Some had the light stronger than others; everybody had it, but nobody seemed to know it except me.

I told no one what I saw or felt. I kept my mouth shut. My dad used to call me "Silent Pete" when I was a kid growing up. After I returned from Bozeman, he started calling me "Silent Pete" again, in a good-natured way, besides, silence was better than a stutter. He was right: I had nothing to say because I had no words to describe what I'd been through. During the year that followed I slowly learned to control my stutter.

≈ 30 ≈

ZooMass

The summer after I returned to Marlborough, Massachusetts, I also returned to my special white pine tree in the woodlands behind my parents' house. There, I practiced my sitting meditation while I leaned against its pitchy rough-barked trunk. I did not date. I did not go out. I worked as a laborer at the same contracting company I'd worked for the summer before. I read literature for escape and kept to myself as much as I could.

In the fall, I went back to UMass Amherst again—ZooMass, as we called it—and enrolled in a pantomime class. My instructor, Jody, had studied under Tony Montanaro, who studied with Marcel Marceau in France. I felt part of quite the artist lineage to be a student in Jody's class. The most important thing, though, was that Jody taught us yoga every day to warm us up for mime. Jody taught us that yoga is not just to stretch and strengthen our body, but it is also to focus our mind and open our soul to God.

That semester I also took a course in the Comparative Literature Department called, "Comparative Mystical Literature East and West." I was hungry for God, who, for me, had no name that could ever be said. I needed more than the traditional church could give me. I needed God directly—not mediated, not tamed, but wild and living, present and experiential. I read so that I might learn if there was anybody, dead or living, who could tell me how to go Home without taking my own life. I needed heaven within me.

It turns out that across the globe, for centuries, men and women whom we call mystics and contemplatives have pursued God, and many of them had written works that described their indescribable experience. I quickly learned that it was much smarter to read the ancient writing of the mystics and contemplatives than it was to read any modern writer on the subject.

My death had left me knowing that God had no form, was no thing, was beyond form, and had created all things, including me. No concept, no idea, no words, could contain God. Therefore, I needed every concept, every idea, and every ancient word to try to make sense of what had happened to me. I have always been a spiritual person. I was spiritual as a child, even mystical, in the ancient sense of the word, as I would later discover in my reading. God had always had a grip on me when I was growing up, and this remains true.

This class opened my eyes to the world of people who, while not exactly like me, were close enough in kind. I began reading many deep and serious spiritual writings from around the globe. I read voraciously, hoping to find anything that might help me understand where I had been and what had happened to me.

The class ended with a voluntary, weekend-long silent retreat at St. Joseph's Abbey. It was at the same Trappist Abbey where my high school religion teacher had learned the meditation practice he'd taught me years before, the practice of which had sustained me. My entire class was invited to attend the retreat along with our professor, a deacon in a Catholic church and practitioner of meditation. He'd begun our class that fall by saying it was a class for serious scholars and that we'd get no credit for navel gazing.

At the retreat, we practiced navel gazing. We sat or walked in silent meditation for the entire weekend. There was no talking at all. The monastery allowed us one visit with the novitiate and guest master, Father Theophane Boyd, who looked a lot like Ichabod Crane dressed in brown and white monk's robes. He was very tall and very skinny, with bony, thin, and prominently knuckled fingers that could probably palm a basketball. His Adam's apple protruded like a Granny Smith and moved up and down his throat whenever he spoke. His hair was gray, long, shaggy, untamable, and stuck out in various directions. His clear blue eyes were like laser beams that read a soul just by looking into another's eyes and penetrating the heart. When he looked at me, my heart caught fire. I could see the fire in him, and I believed he could see it in me.

He spoke about life in the monastery and about spirituality in general terms. During the question and answer period, one of my classmates, David, asked him, "What is it like to be you?" Father Theophane Boyd was seated in front of us, and we were at his feet. He closed his eyes and rocked his upper body back and forth slowly as he considered how to answer. He opened his eyes and said, "I used to be asleep, and now I am awake." This man radiated light. Being in his presence was like being among the illuminated. Being awake, like him, became my goal.

I returned frequently to the monastery in the subsequent years, seeking his counsel and direction. I adopted him as my spiritual advisor, and he tolerated me.

I used to be asleep, and often I wish I could just go back to sleep.

⇜ 31 ⇝

Today

Today, some thirty years later, I sit in Maine in my studio listening to the sound of the sea crashing on the rocks and the nearby foghorn and bell buoy. As I write, a deep and old sadness touches me. It scares me a little. This sadness is familiar and similar to how I felt in those first days and months in 1980. It is a feeling of divergence. I am always in two places at once. It is like I am a river that splits in two, with one branch heading one way, and the other heading another way, giving me not one experience of life but two simultaneously. That feeling never leaves me.

The branch that weaves through life here always changes. The branch that leads to There never changes. *There* feels like a deep truth, a centering of a sort, a love inexplicable; yet, at the same time, it feels like a sad, unrequited love—a love that is always there, but just out of reach. I have this strong desire for the only One who can love me the way I know love can feel. I belong to God.

There are times I wish that was not true, but it is true and I cannot ever escape that. My wife says that has made our marriage difficult. She says it is probably true of all marriages where one partner has died and come back and the other partner has not. I live in a constant state of nonattachment. Not detachment. I am not aloof. I am simply not fully connected here, and that, of course, includes everything, even my marriage.

But I am here. And I am married and have two grown children whom I, like all parents, love more than life itself. I had not planned on having kids, but God had other ideas. I had not planned on marrying, not at least until I met my wife at a meeting in Boston where she was a presenter and I was in the audience. I was working my first real job after UMass as a legislative aide for a Massachusetts representative. She was working for the Massachusetts Department of Health. It was her job to speak with me about pending legislation that mattered to her department. We arranged to meet to discuss it, and I went back to my office and told my representative that I was smitten. He warned me not to mix work and love, but it was too late for that. I asked her out, and on our wedding day my representative forgave my indiscretion of dating someone from work.

Before our wedding it got rather complicated because I was seeking a way into Saint Joseph's Abbey. I had been going on retreat there regularly and had decided that I wanted to be a Trappist monk. It seemed that those monks lived in the light of God, and I craved that light. I felt that I did not fit in this world and that I might fit into the monastery. Falling in love complicated that.

I decided that I would delay a monastic life by going to divinity school for a two-year master's degree with a focus on the history of Christian contemplation and mysticism. As an undergraduate I had already interviewed with Princeton, and so I interviewed at Harvard and Yale. In the end, I chose Yale and planned on continuing my education in a doctoral program after earning my MA. While I was there, the dean of admissions took a shine to me and convinced me to switch to the three-year Master of Divinity degree and to consider joining the United Church of Christ with an aim toward ordination. Upon graduation I was invited to preach at a wider church gathering. After my sermon, a reverend approached me and told me he was seeking an associate minister and he would be pleased if I applied. I did, and landed a three-year extended interim associate minister's job in a suburban New Haven church. I later served four years as a minister and preacher on an island off the coast of Maine, Deer Isle, and then in the resort town of Boothbay Harbor, Maine.

One day years later, in 2001, I told my NDE story publicly for the first time from the pulpit in Boothbay Harbor. I had told it only twice before: once to a dear friend, at divinity school, in 1986, whose face betrayed to me his love, kindness, confusion, and concern for my mental well-being, and who swore secrecy to me; and, previously, on the day before I married my fiancée in 1985.

That first day I shared my story publicly from the pulpit, I needed to try to explain to them why I had done what I had done—and on that day I tried to frame language to describe the indescribable, speak the unspeakable. I had been the minister at the Congregational Church of Boothbay Harbor, Maine, United Church of Christ for about nine years. We recently had ended our very hard times over our decade together, which is putting it kindly and mildly. Over a time period of about thirteen years, a total of $200,000 was stolen from the church where I was pastor, and $3,000 was stolen from me personally. When it became apparent that something was up and I started asking questions, I was personally attacked and very nearly forced out of the church and threatened with being defrocked. A secret cell within the church controlled the board of trustees and the finances and isolated certain deacons and loyal friends, and it nearly destroyed our church and our congregation.

But we succeeded in overcoming and thriving as a body despite what had happened to us. On one Sunday morning, just before church, a parishioner asked me "how my faith had endured unshakably" through a decade of church turmoil. On that Sunday morning in 2001, I knew I did not have any faith, because what near-death experiencer has need of faith when he knows that God is Real? I wondered if I should finally tell my congregation the truth. My faith? I had none. It is a strange thing that I decided on the spur of the moment to finally admit the truth to my parishioners. I decided to tell them the truth about me: I had no faith. I have no faith. I have not had faith of any sort or believed in God ever since that dark March day and night on Lower Weeping Wall in 1980. I decided to come clean and tell my congregation just how it was that I endured nearly a decade of angst, and personal abuse, and trusted God that I would—and that we would—endure and heal, if only the truth were found out and told.

On that Sunday morning, I pondered how I might explain to my people how God is Real, and that while I had no faith, I know that I am known by God, and beloved. I have no faith, because on that night in March of 1980, my faith was taken from me. Before that, I had been a faithful person all of my life, a believer, a Christian by birth and upbringing, and then a born-again Catholic Christian active within the Charismatic youth movement. I had spoken in tongues. I had heard interpretation of tongues at prayer meetings. I had been slain in the spirit. All of that was gone in the blink of an eye and replaced with knowing that I am known by God, and knowing that God is Real. One does not have to believe in what is Real. What is Real is Real; it requires no belief and no faith. I am no longer blind. I no longer have to take the leap of faith I had taken.

So, there I was that Sunday morning, nearly two decades into being a church minister preaching to my congregation about the need for belief and faith, and yet I had none. I faced a choice that morning: tell the truth or lie.

For my part in the healing of this church, I found myself needing, truly feeling compelled for the very first time, to speak aloud my truth, tell my story, and be unafraid of what people might think of me. For decades, I had feared that if I told my story, people would think that I was crazy, insane, or just a fool. That morning, my fear vanished. Suddenly, I no longer cared what people thought of my truth, so I decided to answer this parishioner's question spontaneously, and from the pulpit.

Why then, and why so publicly? It was necessary— because the time was right, and because God had made it impossible for me to ever feel abandoned, to ever feel alone, to ever feel lost in my soul, ever, and that pressure inside me that started on the morning that I had awoken with my stutter had never left me; the internal pressure to speak had only continued to become more and more intense. Since I came back from death, I have not felt alone, not for a moment. Oh, plenty of times I have wanted to feel alone. And plenty of times I have not wanted to feel God as real and present, but I've had no choice in that matter. For that, I've felt lost here on earth and in this world ever since the day I got back. I am lost today. I was lost yesterday. And I know I will be lost tomorrow. I am displaced. I am alien. I am not from here . . . but, then again, neither are you. The only difference is that I know I am not from here. Unless you have died and come back, you do not know. Trust me, God is Real; you will go Home, and it is beautiful.

The night I died has always felt like a blessing and a curse: The blessing is that I know I can never escape the sight of God; yet, that is the curse too. I do not believe this. I know it. There is a difference between believing and knowing. I *know* where Home is, and I long for it. That night on the mountain I learned that I had a new Home, which was my old Home, my first Home, my only Home, my real Home, and that Home is the one and only deep desire of my heart. (And, that is why it is difficult to love a near-death experience survivor—my heart fully belongs to another.)

My wife is a saint—patient, tolerant, understanding. She understands and accepts that she will always be second in my heart. I wish it were not so, but it is. Although I love her and my children, my heart is over there, on the other side. My Home is heaven. It is your Home too. It is where I am from and to where I am going when I die again. It was promised to me.

So, I told my congregation about my lack of faith that Sunday morning, instead of preaching the sermon I'd prepared with over twenty hours of work—reading, research, writing, and editing. I told them because I felt they needed to know why I hadn't quit in the midst of the worst of our church's turmoil, and why during one of the darkest times of my life, I continued to pray, and actually dove even deeper into God. Why? Because God is all there is to me. God gives me strength even in my weakness.

I waved my sermon manuscript in the air and said, "I prepared a sermon for today. It took half of my week to prepare it, and here it is. But I am not going to preach this today. This morning, just before church, I was asked how I had endured terrible treatment here while we sought to solve the problem of our finances and discovered it was actually embezzlement. How did I endure? Let me tell you a story. This is the first time I am going to tell this story, and truly I don't want to tell it, but I feel I must. I kept a secret for twenty years. But if you want to know the truth about my strong faith, well, the truth is, I don't have any faith. Here is why . . ."

I then began telling my tale aloud to an attentive crowd who loved me, and in whose presence I felt safe enough to tell the truth of how I lost my faith and gained a love of God. That day, and every day since whenever I have told my story—and I have told it hundreds of times to audiences small and large—the hardest part of the telling is explaining my journey to the other side. I went through the fire once, and I expect to pass through the fire again.

On the other side, there is no time. Time does not exist. Time exists here. Time moves forward here, and we can look back in history and think about time. Time is entwined in nature, in the physics of this three-dimensional world. In time, there is a sequence of events. Here, one thing happens, and then the next thing happens, and then the next. On the other side time does not exist. Nothing happens in sequence. So, did everything happen all at once to me there? I do not know. It is eternity over there. Not forever. Forever is a measure of time. Eternity is outside of time.

Furthermore, as I have said before and will say again, there are no words, no things, no body, no brain, no culture, no history, and no language. Here, in this world, in our world of height, depth, width, and time, there are things. Everything here is a *thing*, including this book, and you, and me, and rocks, hills, words, brains, molecules, particles—even the Higgs boson is a thing. Everything is a *thing* here.

On the other side, there are no things. No *thing* exists there. No time. No things. Nothing. No thing. The most difficult task in telling this part of the story, the most important part of my entire story, is finding words to describe the indescribable. Words are things, too. Words describe things; words are symbols of things. We often think in words; and, more often, we think in symbols and images, emotions and memories, and they are all *things*. I am belaboring this point to make a point: Heaven and God are indescribable. Yet, I feel the fire within me to describe what cannot be described. It is weird to be me. I'm sure of that. For anybody who has died, crossed over, and come back to life here in this world, life is strange, and alien.

These days, I serve God on broadcast and cable television, FM radio, and social media as a sacred storyteller in Maine and beyond as the minister of First Radio Parish Church of America (DailyDevotions.org). God has given me a media platform to speak the truth that God is Real and Love is Real and that in dying we find life. From the first morning after my near-death experience I have felt an inner compulsion to tell about it. I locked that compulsion inside me, but in there it grew stronger and stronger, and demanded to be told, but I was a rebellious sort, and refused. I feel that I must tell it now.

It doesn't make me feel good to tell it. To tell it I have to go back into the dark places in my life. Telling my story usually makes me cry. I wish it didn't, but it does. I tell it to give hope. I tell it because God compels me to tell it. I am driven to tell it. I think that this story is one among many that are coming from the near-death community meant to raise the sight of the world to love, to give hope to the dying, and comfort to the mourning.

I am humbled by my situation, and I hope that the messenger is never confused with the message. I am an imperfect and broken person; only God is whole and holy. Love is what I preach, and I pray for and hunt for that full feeling of Love I experienced when I was in heaven. It is always there, filling me, yet also just out of reach. Though I immediately forgot most of what I knew and understood about life and love once I came back to this world and my body—I still sense that what I know now, today, about heaven is a mere fragment, a shard, of what I knew there—experiencing it left me with a desire for the One, a drive for God, and so I strive to open my heart as wide as I can and shout in prayer, "God, here I am. Notice me!" I know that I am noticed. It feels that way, but it is just a tiny fraction of what I knew on the other side, just a droplet that I feel. What I want is to be immersed in the river.

～ 32 ～

Being Here and Going There

I am often asked if dying and coming back influenced my decision to get ordained. The answer is yes and no. In some ways, I have always been on this path. I've had a strong interior spiritual call since I was a young boy. I'm sort of an accidental clergy member; I did not intend to remain at the pulpit, but I kept finding work that had to be done, so I did it. Also, the intensity of my spirituality increased dramatically after my near-death experience, and I knew of no other way I could get away with spending hours each day in yoga and meditation and call it work. The work of ministry has allowed me the honor of sitting and conversing with many who are dying, and many who have died. And I feel better equipped to help because of my experience.

The best part of my ministry job has always been sitting with the dying—talking, praying, and simply being with them, being real, authentic, and truthful. I've found that, when I've shared my story, even if very briefly, expressing my assurance of eternal life, my hope, my knowing that I am known, has helped ease hundreds into death, and into Love-Hope-Joy-Beauty-Truth-Charity-Kindness-Compassion-Love-Patience-Beauty-Love.

I have been an unconventional pastor because I am an unconventional person, one who has at times run afoul of certain parishioners who had their own ideas of clerical propriety and dignity. I have never been good at either of those things. Inevitably, some of these parishioners have become gravely ill, and—whether they like it or not, whether I liked them or not—it has been and will be my duty to visit them and help their passage across. Once someone reaches the stage where he or she sees death coming, we have become the fastest of friends.

I said it was an honor to sit with the dying, and it has been, every time. Part of this is because people often become more honest in their deaths; but more so, as the time nears, it is because the veil that hides heaven from the eyes of humans sometimes begins to lift. In the old days, when Auntie Mabel was dying, she might say, "I see an angel" or "I see my husband (or my mother)." The attendant might say, "No, dear. There is no angel here," or "No, dear. Your mother (or your husband) has been dead for ten years. She (or he) is not here." These days, nurses, doctors, and clergy just let those who are dying express what they believe they are seeing, even if no one else can see it. Who is to say that what they see is not real, and that an angel or a deceased family member is not in the room? The veil between heaven and earth is lifted more often than we know.

For weeks after a funeral, it has been my job to visit the grieving mother, widow, husband, or child. Often, in hushed tones, they would lean across the kitchen table and say words such as these: "Peter, this is going to sound crazy. This morning when I came down for breakfast, there was Tom, standing right there by the sink with his back to me. I was shocked. He turned around, looked me in the eyes, and said, 'Don't worry, dear. I am okay. I'll see you again.' He smiled and then vanished." A hundred times or more, I've heard such stories from the grieving. Maybe you have a similar story or have heard one like it. If the afterlife is real, and I am here to tell you that it is, then why wouldn't your loved one want to tell you that she or he is okay and all is well?

If you are dying right now, or fear dying, or love someone who is dying, then please, let me tell you this: You are not your body. You are your soul. Your soul inhabits your body. When you go across, or when the one you love departs, the soul does not die. Only the body dies. The real you does *not* die. When you die, you will carry with you—yourself—the *you* who is you, plus all the love you have given away or shared, and all the love you have gathered. All the bits and pieces of love you have given or collected are in your soul right now, and they are yours to keep. They are your treasure. Jesus said, "Store up treasure for yourself in heaven, where moths and rust cannot destroy and thieves do not break in and steal" (Matthew 6:20). He was right. Every act of love accumulates in your soul. No one, and nothing, can take these from you or destroy them. Love is eternal, and love is inside you.

You also get to carry all the pain you have caused, and whether you choose to believe me or not, that pain is sin. We all sin. I still sin, probably every day; but I love every day, too, and I know that God is merciful and forgiving—thank God.

You will carry your memories, your self, your mind, and your soul into heaven, a heaven where there is no pain, no boredom, no suffering, and where there is love and beauty beyond comprehension. God is all-loving and knows you thoroughly already, from before you were born, even before you were knit in your mother's womb. God created your innermost being. God knew you, and knows you (Jeremiah 1:5; Psalm 139:13).

You are loved. You are beloved in particular. You have always been loved; you will always be loved. You are loved with a love beyond imagination, with a power of love beyond comprehension, a thousand times sweeter than the sweetest love you have ever felt. Love is how you were made. Love is how you exist. You will not end. When the trumpet blows for you, you will transform in the twinkling of an eye (1 Corinthians 15:52) and find yourself in the presence of God, who is Love and Mercy and Truth and Beauty. Be prepared to be loved and to be welcomed: you are going Home. Death is only a doorway. When your time comes, as it must, walk through that doorway and love God. Trust God. Believe. That's all you have to do—simply believe. You can believe in God, because God is Real. This life is simply one bridge in between.

My job is to bring hope. I hope you have hope now. God is Real. Heaven is Real. God is LOVE. We are not from here; we are from There. Our end is our beginning. We go back to where we came from. This life is simply one bridge in between.

Do we all go to heaven? That is not my call, nor is it yours. That choice is God's, the Loving, the Merciful, the Forgiving. I certainly think so—or, at least, I think we all get the chance. I am rather sure I got in because I was ashamed of the pain that I'd caused, but mostly because God is forgiving.

It is true that all is well. All has always been well. All will be well. It is true that all is well because God is Love, and life is but a wink of God's eye.

My desire to die has abated some in recent years. This is not to say I was ever suicidal; I was not. Philippians 1:23–24 probably says it best for me: "I am hard pressed between the two: my desire is to depart and be with Christ, for that is far better; but to remain in the flesh is more necessary for you." 2 Corinthians 5:8 conveys my point well: "Yes, we do have confidence, and we would rather be away from the body and at home with the Lord."

From where I stand, human beings are made of at least two parts—the body and the spirit/soul. The parts are connected to each other in this world, but unconnected in the next. In this world, through prayer, through meditation, we can access the spirit/soul and learn of its existence; we can empty ourselves of ourselves and get out of the way of God, out of the way of God's grace/love, so it can infuse us and lift us. Why the wait? Not because of any purity of ours, or because of our meditative focus, but because only God can do it. Our job is to get out of the way.

That is what meditation does. Meditation teaches that I am at my best when I am at my least. Meditation gets me out of the way. Meditation fills the belly with light. It's like gathering a thin silken thread of light, then winding that into a cocoon inside my belly. Every day, I wind more thread onto my spool, and during the day I can unwind it to give it away. Meditation is like sipping from a bottomless cup and swallowing the water of life, which fills a reservoir in my belly, giving me a bellyful each day—and then, I give the water away. The water gives me strength. It shows me the way. It reminds me that I am not from here. I long for the day when I will finally get to return Home.

Meditation simply opens the inner door, over and over and over, and lets the Light seep in. As for God's part, God can swing open wide the door and let in all the Light we can stand within us, within the human body, and not shatter from joy. Or, God can swing wide open our inner door and lift us through heavens even unto God himself, in a beatific vision of God, or near enough to see the Light or hear the music that sings the soul into being. We need not die to be lifted to God, but it helps. Dying is the shortest route Home; it opens the door the widest. It is a door that rarely swings both ways. Usually, it is one-way, and it closes behind us.

What form of meditation should you practice? The one that is rooted to your faith tradition. In this life, in this world, we can open our door to God through prayer, community, kindness, and love in action in a thousand small ways or a thousand large ways. All of these allow us to get out of God's way, allow God's Light and Love to seep into us, and into the world. God is Real. God is Love. God loves you, personally and particularly.

Where are you from? You are from where I'm from—heaven and God. I am not from here, and neither are you. We are both, we are all, from heaven—every human being upon this planet. Heaven is our beginning, and heaven is our end. We are souls first, and bodies second. We belong to God, who is Light and Love, Mercy, Joy, and Beauty beyond belief, beyond imagination.

God is Love. God is Love. God is Love. Death is a door. All is well. All has always been well. All will be well. All will always be well—because of God's Love. Never forget that.

Mount Madison summit. Presidential Range, White Mountain National Forest, New Hampshire, October 2010. Photograph by Don Scott.

Acknowledgments

My tolerant and loving wife, Michelle, deserves the most thanks. She has endured years of my eccentricities that come from being a near-death experiencer. My two children, Lexa and Andy, also deserve honor and praise for having endured a dad for whom death and dying are regular dinner conversation and for having the misfortune of having been raised as pastor's kids in a small town through no fault of their own.

I am grateful to my literary agent, Stephany Evans of FinePrint Literature, who put up with my peccadillos for months upon months while working with me on my proposal and for shopping it around until she found the right publisher.

Thanks to Greg Brandenburg, associate publisher at Hampton Roads, who read my manuscript straight through one Saturday morning and then took a chance on me. Big thanks to my copyeditor, Susie Pitzen, who makes me appear to be a better writer than I am.

I'd like to thank my board of trustees at First Radio Parish Church of America/DailyDevotions.org for allowing me the time I needed to write this book and Lorraine Lamont, who helped with early copyediting.

And my friends, who loved me and tolerated me when I was lost and trying to figure out what had happened to me even though I did not tell them what had happened: Don S., Steve M., Steve C., Douglas G., Kerri K., Rhanda J., Bill L., and Charlie C.

About the Author

Peter Baldwin Panagore earned his BA in English from the University of Massachusetts and a MDiv from Yale University. He was ordained in the United Church of Christ and served churches in suburban Connecticut and Maine. He is the writer, on-air talent, and host of a daily two-minute broadcast on two Gannett Company-owned NBC stations in Maine, reaching an audience of 350,000 a week. He is the fifth minister of First Radio Parish Church of America (founded in 1926). Visit Peter online at www.dailydevotion.com.